I0049319

SHATTER

— THE —

GLASS

CEILING

SEVEN KEYS TO SUCCESS FOR WOMEN AND PEOPLE OF COLOR

VINITIA MATHEWS, PhD

Copyright © 2024 by Vinitia Mathews

All rights reserved. No part of this publication may be reproduced, distributed, or transmitted in any form or by any means, including photocopying, recording, or other electronic or mechanical methods, without the prior written permission of the publisher, except in the case of brief quotations embodied in critical reviews and certain other noncommercial uses permitted by copyright law.

The events and conversations in this book have been set down to the best of the author's ability, although some names and details have been changed to protect the privacy of individuals.

Title: Shatter the glass ceiling
Subtitle: Seven keys to success for women and people of color
Author name: Vinitia Mathews
Description: First edition

ISBN: 979-8-9918547-0-2 (Hardcover)
ISBN: 979-8-9918547-1-9 (Paperback)
ISBN: 979-8-9918547-2-6 (e book)

Library of Congress Control Number: 2024922649

www.shattertheglassceilingbook.com
www.sageleadersolutions.com

Printed in the United States of America

With Deep Gratitude

Contents

Introduction

It is lonely being a woman and a person of color in the professional world.

We have all encountered the glass ceiling—those invisible barriers faced by women and minorities in the workplace, which hold us back and limit our potential to succeed. I was inspired to write this book to ensure those of you like me—women and people of color—understand that you are not alone in the career challenges you face, and that there are actionable steps you can take to overcome them. In my own career, I have not only faced the glass ceiling, but I've also had great success shattering it.

I have served as both an officer and senior vice president of multibillion-dollar for-profit organizations, and been a key operational leader within publicly traded, private, private equity-owned, and nonprofit systems. I have two decades of healthcare operational experience and a decade of experience as a management consultant and executive leadership coach serving multiple industries. I have led multidisciplinary teams with multimillion-dollar budgets and been instrumental in creating inclusive cultures in organizations ranging from ten thousand to over fifty thousand employees across multiple states.

But getting past the barriers to success was not an easy or simple process. I found throughout my career that the more I excelled and the higher I rose; I was surrounded by fewer and fewer people who looked like me. As I climbed the organizational ladder and became more successful, the more alone I felt. Once I faced a myriad of challenges to get to where I was, I assessed my peers and noticed that few around me shared my perspectives or had faced similar challenges. I became aware of executive meetings and events that my white male peers attended, but to which I received no invitations. The peers who attended these "closed" meetings and events would reminisce about things they'd said and done while there. They appeared to have a special bonding time with the executives because of those shared experiences and, as such, seemed to benefit since those peers were top-of-mind for promotions and key opportunities. It is an awful feeling to know you have been denied access to an exclusive club which would have opened doors to upward organizational mobility.

I turned to books and podcasts, searching for solutions. I couldn't find any information to help me deal with the challenges I was facing, nor was I able to find specific solutions or actions I could take to overcome them. I had to figure things out the hard way or seek support beyond the walls in which I worked because as a woman of color there was no one like me to turn to in the leadership of those organizations. Later in my career, when I became an executive leadership coach, it was striking to see that many of the challenges I had faced and had to overcome were still being faced by clients who were women and/or people of color. For this reason, my goal as an executive leadership coach became helping women and people of color.

To this day, there are still very few published resources out there that offer specific career advice for women or people of color. I was inspired to do something to change that situation. I have been highly impactful as a coach serving external clients, as well as internal clients in the organizations in which I worked. My former clients include executives, physicians, clinicians, attorneys, middle managers, women as well as men, and people of color as well as white clients. I wrote this book to share some of the wisdom I give my clients, to make your career success journey an easier one than mine has been, and to give you strength and encouragement so you know you are not alone in what you face.

Drawing upon my career experiences as well as those of my coaching clients, you will learn actionable steps to overcome challenges, and ways to develop skills to enhance your career success, no matter the industry or role where you currently reside. It is my sincere hope that by sharing this wisdom, I will save you career angst and help to accelerate your career success.

How do you know whether you would benefit from following the guidance outlined in this book?

- If you are the first member of your family to go to college, this book is for you.

- If English is not the primary language spoken in your home, this book is for you.

- If you have been told you have an accent, this book is for you.

- If you had to pay for your own university education (whether through scholarships, by working, or securing loans), this book is for you.

- If you don't have an Ivy League or tier one university education, this book is for you.

- If you support anyone other than yourself financially, this book is for you.

- If you are one of the only women or one of the only people of color in your workplace, this book is for you.

If one or more of the above statements apply to you, the "normal" rules of career advancement typically won't work for you. We women and people of color have faced and are facing unique experiences that have not burdened others. Because they were not first-generation college educated, they were able to ask their parents and grandparents for advice about navigating and excelling in the education system; they often have family friends who can open doors for them professionally; they don't have the financial burden of repaying student loans; they don't have the constant pressure of supporting others in their family financially; and they haven't had to pay the emotional toll of being "the only" at work. These financial and emotional tolls may have set us back, and now we need every possible advantage to charge forward. This book is filled with advice and tactics to help accelerate your career journey. If you don't aspire to a leadership position or currently lead a team, don't worry, the advice in this book will still help with your career success.

In each chapter, we will explore a key leadership skill or challenge that either accelerated or set back my professional journey or impacted the careers of my coaching clients. You will read about developing tenacity, exuding positivity, honing your competencies, building a robust support system, establishing and maintaining boundaries, harnessing fear, and being authentic to yourself. To help you recognize the career challenges and "speed bumps" you might encounter, each chapter includes stories and examples. Each chapter also contains actionable tips and suggestions and ends with a reflection section. By the time you reach the end of this book, you will be able to take specific action to accelerate your career success and shatter any glass ceiling that might be holding you back.

As you read the book, I highly recommend keeping track of your thoughts, ideas, questions, and concerns. Make yourself a commitment to improve your situation by documenting your thoughts in the allocated space at the end of each chapter. It is important that you "listen" to and document your own reflections as you work through this book. Listening to and documenting your own thoughts is a key part of your transformative experience. To make the best use of these notes to yourself, it is essential that you periodically look back and assess how much you have grown and progressed in your career to keep yourself motivated to do the things that have aided your success, and keep working on ways to overcome what may still constrain your success.

You are not alone! Something inspired you to pick up this book at this time in your career. May my words provide you with the encouragement to transform your leadership and career success. May this book provide you with the specific tools and tactics you need to help you shatter the glass ceiling!

Chapter One

Developing Tenacity

As a woman or person of color, tenacity is an imperative trait for your career success. Tenacity is the ability to keep going, even after failure and setbacks. As a woman or person of color, you will face roadblocks that others don't have to face. Your failures may be judged more harshly, and you may even have to face blatant acts of sabotage in your career. Without tenacity, you won't have the motivation or energy to pick yourself up and keep moving forward.

We women and people of color have faced and are facing unique challenges in our careers. One of the most ubiquitous examples is the emotional toll of being "the only" at work. As "the only" we are expected to conform to norms of the majority, often without our own voice or concerns being heard. Others cannot know how isolating and different it feels to be "the only" because they may never have experienced it—they are typically surrounded by people who look like them, have had similar experiences as them, and have similar perspectives as them. We women and people of color typically find ourselves in work settings where those around us don't look like us, don't have experiences that are comparable to ours, and don't share perspectives like ours. There is an emotional toll to feeling like we don't fully belong with those around us. Without tenacity, that emotional toll could crush and defeat us.

Women and people of color may see problems differently than those around us, and perhaps for that reason, we may come up with unique solutions that aren't widely accepted in the workplace. If such alternative views are seen as riskier, the degree of support garnered by others can help mitigate the risk of our recommendations. But the support we receive depends on our organization's culture and how well we are received. Organizational cultures that aren't open to alternative views will shoot down views that don't match the status quo. If we work in a culture like that, it can be disheartening to feel like our ideas and recommendations do not matter. It can be soul-crushing to have ideas and recommendations repeatedly shot down. And it will require tremendous courage and tenacity to speak up after being repeatedly shot down.

There is a common thread among my clients who are women and people of color—they express frustration and weariness about not feeling like they fully belong in their workplaces; they express frustration about not being fully heard; they express frustration about having to speak up and raise alternative perspectives; and they express frustration about not feeling fully supported by those around them.

During coaching sessions, while we work together to achieve their coaching career goals, we also do very intentional work to acknowledge the tenacity they have demonstrated thus far in their professional work. This is essential because acknowledging and recognizing how tenacious you have been in the past will fuel your tenacity for the future. Knowing you are not starting from zero on the tenacity scale will make your goal of developing even more tenacity seem that much more achievable and within reach. When working on developing your tenacity, think of your tenacity glass as being half-full, not completely empty.

Perseverance is a central concept of tenacity. And one important facet of developing perseverance is to have a hopeful and optimistic mindset regardless of the problem being faced. That hopeful and optimistic mindset is what allows you to believe the problem can be overcome. An optimistic person's positive outlook creates momentum which allows them to persevere by taking action when they face a problem. And that momentum fuels them further even if they have to try multiple times to overcome the problem or have to use a variety of strategies to do so. Those positive experiences help a person strengthen their perseverance. In the future, when they face another setback, because they innately believe the problem they face can be solved, they view that setback as merely temporary. They simply have "not yet" found the right solution to overcome the problem.

Let me share a little about my own upbringing to further clarify the concept of tenacity. I grew up in Zambia, a developing nation in sub-Saharan Africa, as the third child of Indian parents who moved to Africa soon after their marriage. Poverty is relative to the local socioeconomic environment particularly in a developing nation, so while I consciously opt not to use the word poor, our family was far from rich. Well before I was a teenager, I knew I wanted more options than a university education in Zambia would afford me. My best options for higher education appeared to be India, the United Kingdom, or the United States, based on the successes of others I'd seen around me. Our infrequent family trips to India clearly showed me I was a foreigner in that land—I didn't understand the cultural norms and inadvertently violated them; I was illiterate in all Indian languages; and I could only communicate verbally, albeit poorly.

The one trip I made to the United Kingdom during my childhood was memorable for the wrong reasons: While walking in a residential neighborhood, I was called a "Paki" by a white stranger and advised to "go back to my own country." The fact that a total stranger thought it was acceptable to verbally attack a teenager harmlessly walking on the street made it clear to me that I wouldn't do well in a country with such blatant racism. Conversely, when I visited the United States as a teenager, I fell in love with the country and its friendly, welcoming people! Everywhere I went during that visit, I found Americans to be open and welcoming, quick to smile and laugh, and effusive with their manners.

It was during my visit to the US that I decided I would pursue a university education in this country. I made that decision, knowing fully well that my parents couldn't afford to pay for my education. This was a dilemma. International students are ineligible for US loans and are not permitted to work off-campus. If I was going to make an American university education a reality, somehow, I would have to get past the financial setback.

Growing up in a developing nation, one is constantly faced with setbacks. Things that are straightforward and have simple solutions in the industrialized world may not be options in a developing nation. Setbacks were nothing new to me. And like most who grow up in a developing nation, when faced with roadblocks, I looked for ways to get over, under, or around them. Giving up due to a roadblock was simply not an option. While I didn't have the means to pay for a university education in the US, I was still determined to get my education there. I struck a deal with my parents—if they would pay for my first year of university, I'd figure out how to pay for the rest on my own.

At the age of seventeen, I arrived in the US to begin my university education. I didn't know how I was going to pay for school beyond the first year. I just knew I was determined to do so. When I arrived on campus, I began searching earnestly for every financial opportunity available to me. I was fortunate and blessed to be offered a job that would pay half my tuition, starting in my second semester. I also worked extremely hard academically and, based on grades from my first semester, landed a scholarship that paid the other half of my tuition for the second semester onwards. Tenacity enabled me to secure full tuition benefits for my entire degree, within only a few months after I arrived in the country!

Over the next few years, I had many more opportunities to demonstrate tenacity. As I pursued two graduate degrees (I was continuing my education as an international student, therefore I was still unable to secure loans or work off-campus), there were years when I couldn't afford to eat more than one meal a day. That memory and experience still sit with me to this day—keeping me grounded and compassionate. Those times were tough, but what got me through was the knowledge that they would not last forever. I knew once I got my final degree, the PhD would allow me to get a job and have a better financial future.

Your experience may not be the same as mine. But undoubtedly you have had to persevere to overcome obstacles to get to where you are in your career. Perhaps you have had to work multiple jobs to help support your family, denying you time to focus on your own education. Perhaps you grew up in an unsafe neighborhood and constant vigilance to protect your physical safety impacted how you had to navigate to get safely to and from school/

work. Whatever your experience, reflect on what inspired you to persevere despite obstacles and hardships.

Many of my coaching clients who are women express the hardship of juggling a family while pursuing their career. They share how difficult it is not to spend as much time with their loved ones as they would like; they also comment that they feel they are unable to perform at their best at work because of family demands and expectations; I hear their sense of guilt that they are shortchanging both their loved ones and their work teams because of all the demands on their time. None of these challenges may appear unique to women. Indeed, many men may feel the same hardships of balancing work and family demands. However, what certainly makes it harder for women is that in most industries there is a lack of representation of women who have successfully juggled both a family and a comparable career trajectory. There are numerous studies showing the higher up you go in organizations, the lower the percentage of women represented—a concept coined the leaky pipeline. Even in healthcare where women make up 75 percent of the workforce, only 5 to 15 percent of the executives are women, depending on which study you read. Simply stated, there may be very few female role models who have achieved both professional and personal success.

Compounding the issue is that many of the women who are in those executive roles have structured support to allow them to juggle personal/professional success. That structured support may take the form of a full-time nanny, housekeeping/chef support, or a stay-at-home partner. For the average career woman, obtaining similar structured support may simply be out of financial reach. It will take perseverance and tenacity to endure the hardship of managing personal/professional demands without enough support. With these clients, our coaching work centers around exploring ways to ask for and receive help at home and at work, exploring ways to build in time for their own rest and rejuvenation, and most importantly, getting them to acknowledge how tenacious they are and have been to get to this point in their lives. Simply having the time to focus on themselves and vent/strategize during our coaching sessions can be priceless for my clients.

My coaching clients of color often speak about the hardship and emotional toll of being "the only" at work. They recount stories of not feeling like they belong, not being treated like one of the group, not having their voices heard, and not being seen. Some clients share stories about their ideas repeatedly being dismissed or shut down, and the emotional toll that takes on their confidence and self-worth. They report that when they propose an idea it is dismissed but that when the exact same idea is later proposed by a white peer, it gets a favorable response. They share examples of when their specific needs are not considered which makes them feel invisible and unimportant—such as companies that choose to host their professional events in country clubs that have historically restricted access to minorities, or ordering BBQ pork for meals during professional events which leaves few options for vegetarians and Muslims. From my coaching clients of color, I also hear something I have experienced first-hand— not being invited to join after-work events. It's such a horrible feeling to hear others recount how much they loved one of those events when you were not even invited. To move forward positively, you will need to put aside those negative feelings and find ways to build yourself back up. You need to focus on your tenacity!

How to Develop Tenacity - Flex Your Tolerance for Discomfort

One way I developed my "tenacity" muscle was to push the boundaries of my comfort zone by intentionally learning new skills. Now I use the same process in my work with coaching clients to help them do the same. When we are in new situations and we have to learn completely new skills, it creates immense self-confidence! Once we begin learning the new skill and move from a novice to being able to survive or even master that skill, it develops emotional fortitude and the knowledge that you will be able to survive other unknown challenges equally successfully. Being a novice while you learn a new skill also means you have to be humble enough to make mistakes and learn from setbacks. In our professional careers, being able to learn from setbacks *and* keep moving forward is an invaluable skill for success. I have had clients who got caught in the quicksand of their setbacks. Our work together centered on getting them to move past the experience by finding ways to learn and grow from it. You can either let the experience of a setback consume and constrain your professional momentum, or you can address it strategically, learn from the experience, and move forward.

To illustrate how I have pushed my own comfort boundaries, let me share a couple of examples. The first is skydiving. As a young child, I used to dream I could fly. Those dreams were full of joy and exuberance and the feeling of complete freedom. When I reached the mid-stage of my career, I felt like I was running on autopilot and needed to shake things up, so I decided to try skydiving. I chose to go solo on my very first jump, rather than jump tethered to a tandem instructor. In retrospect, I suggest folks start with tandem, then progress to solo, but either way, I highly recommend skydiving!

The skydiving training course for my first solo jump was an all-day affair. The instructors were serious and very intense—our lives would literally be in our own hands. The instructors made sure we were adequately skilled to successfully exit the plane, pull our own ripcord for our parachute (instructors will not pull a chute for a student), diagnose whether the deployed chute was "good" (free of tangles), fly the canopy back to the drop zone, and then safely land within the drop zone. The day was fraught with anxiety and fear, but I stayed focused on my goal of completing the dive.

When we boarded the plane late that afternoon, my fear escalated to a nausea-inducing level, but I kept breathing and stayed focused on my goal to complete the dive. When the plane door was opened at 14,000 feet, and it was my turn to scooch up to the open door, my logical brain shut down and the training took over. That first jump was the most terrifying and most exhilarating thing I have ever experienced in my life! And it was such a momentous jump that immediately after I landed, I signed up to become a certified solo skydiver. Subsequent levels and jumps towards solo certification were just as intense and humbling— I learned so much about what I was capable of, including being able to push past huge amounts of fear! The entire skydiving experience enhanced my tenacity and has served me well during my career. Whenever I encountered fear professionally, I would say to myself, *this is not a life-or-death situation, unlike skydiving. It is not the end of the world. You can do this.*

A second example of how I have pushed beyond my comfort zone is by attending racing school on a professional racetrack, using my own street car. In my class, the majority of students were white men with extremely high-powered cars (think Ferraris, Porsches, and Lamborghinis). I was driving a BMW station wagon at the time and overheard the men snickering at my vehicle, but I consciously stayed focused on my goal of completing the course. Each student was assigned an instructor who rode in the passenger seat during the course, so they could coach and assess us in real time.

I am happy to share that I kicked butt that day! While the men had higher horsepower vehicles than mine, I had better technique on the curves and had a better understanding of the "racing line" by listening closely to my instructor's coaching. At the end of the day, my instructor, who was also the owner of the racing school, told the class I was in the top 3 to 5 percent of students he had ever seen because I listened to his coaching and didn't assume driving on a racetrack would be the same as driving on the street. I walked away from this experience with expanded self-confidence.

The racing school experience was more similar to my career than I realized until much later. At the start of the class I felt out of place. I was the only person of color in the class, and one of a small handful of women. I also felt "less than" the men in the class because my car didn't have nearly as much horsepower as theirs did. Additionally, they all had beautiful sports cars while I had a station wagon. These were visible ways I felt inferior. What I did have, unbeknownst to me until the end of the day, was probably the most skilled instructor at the school. Had I not listened intently to his coaching, had I not been humble enough to be willing to learn even though I had been driving all my life, and had I not stayed focused on the goal of successfully completing the course despite feeling inferior, the day would not have been such a success. I learned so many great life lessons from that one experience. The racing experience enhanced my tenacity!

How Flexing Your Tolerance for Discomfort Helps Professionally

As your career progresses, you will often find that you are asked to take on additional responsibilities that expand the scope of your job. Many times, that scope will be beyond your current realm of expertise. The rationale is that your leaders see how well you have led your current team and managed your current duties to achieve excellence, and they want you to do the same with other teams/duties. As a woman or person of color, I encourage you to be willing to say yes to uncertainty! Do your due diligence when considering new opportunities. Contemplate and strategize how a new opportunity might help you achieve your goals or align you with powerful influencers, seek the advice of a trusted advisor/coach, and then step fully into the new opportunity confidently and with optimism.

In my own career, with each successive promotion, I was asked to lead additional team members and take on additional scope beyond my area of expertise. Early in my career, the first time I was asked to take on additional responsibility, it was without the promise of a promotion or even a pay increase. However, I had been wanting to have more influence and impact in my career, and I saw the opportunity as a way to potentially meet those goals and align me with the executive in charge of that area. I knew from my leadership studies that saying yes had the potential to open career doors, even if I didn't know how. There was great uncertainty about what the new role would entail because the role had never existed in the company. I had to work through all the negative thoughts in my head: how would I structure the role given I had never done anything like it? How would I lead company efforts without any formal authority and what if I didn't succeed? I worked through the fears using my past successes and my optimism and faith to get me through. While I did have fears about taking the role, I knew I would regret passing up the chance to succeed at the new opportunity. The fear of looking back with regret for turning down the role far outweighed the fear of taking on the role, so I jumped into the new role wholeheartedly.

That first unstructured role was the launch of big things happening in my career! Had I not been willing to step into the unknown, my career would have taken a very different path. In fact, because of that role, my career progression leapfrogged peers from my previous department. It was a tangible example of what others have called "creating your own luck." Saying yes to uncertainty, in the words of Louise Hay, allowed me to manifest future successes. This powerful lesson early in my career helped increase my tolerance for uncertainty and increased my willingness to take on new challenges. It is a lesson I share with clients. And this lesson is not unique to me. Studies show that the most successful entrepreneurs don't view risk the same way as others—they see new ventures as opportunities to succeed and learn. They know even if a venture "fails," something meaningful will be obtained by going through the experience. I encourage you to be willing to say yes to uncertainty!

Reflection Questions for Developing Tenacity

Tenacity is the ability to keep going, even after failure and setbacks. As a woman or person of color, you will face roadblocks that others don't have to face, and your failures may be judged more harshly. Without tenacity, you won't have the motivation or energy to pick yourself up and keep moving forward. Acknowledging and recognizing how tenacious you have been in the past will fuel your tenacity for the future.

- What are some specific experiences in your life where you demonstrated tenacity?

- What did you learn about yourself and about others from those challenges?

- If you have had any personal or professional setbacks, what did you learn about yourself from each of these scenarios?

Chapter Two

Exuding Positivity

People who exude positivity, or positive energy, have an air of confidence, a can-do quality that influences those around them to perceive them as potential stars. Exuding positivity means that no matter the reality you currently face, you continue to have a positive, optimistic perspective about how things will work out. It means even in those times when you are uncertain, you are able to manage and temper that uncertainty. It means projecting confidence even when you might have imposter syndrome—feeling like a phony despite past successes; or feeling unworthy of a project or role. If you can train yourself to recognize the physical signs that you're feeling uncertain or unworthy, you also can train yourself to snap out of those feelings and focus instead on consciously exuding positivity. Doing so will make others believe in your potential, which is the key to your career success. According to Ready (2010), results get you promoted early in your career, but it is specific behavior that later keeps you on the company's high potential radar. In fact, as your career progresses, it is behavior that matters more and more. One such behavior which I have found to be key in every organization in which I have worked and studied is exuding positivity.

There is a logical reason to exude positivity. Studies show that when equally qualified candidates are evaluated, hiring managers tend to hire the one they *like* the best. Can anything be done to increase your chances of being liked? Yes! Exuding positivity attracts other people to you because people are drawn to positive energy. The concept of energy contagion suggests people feel better after they spend time with those who are positive. Develop the ability to exude positivity and you will hear folks say that being around you always makes them feel better.

We cannot like what we do not know. In fact, when we encounter unknown groups or situations, it is normal to stay neutral while we assess how we feel. In organizations where the hiring managers may not have worked much with women or with people of color, candidates who are female or of color are at a disadvantage because they fall into that "unknown" category. It is important, especially during hiring/selection processes, that you exude positivity to level the playing field and give yourself the best chance possible.

But it is more than just getting hiring managers to like you. It is also about making them comfortable making decisions or choices they may not have made before, or made with much frequency, in the past. In other words, hiring managers may be hesitant to hire someone who is unlike anyone they have hired before. Employment statistics of women and people of color, especially at senior leader levels, show that women and people of color are not hired at the same rates as their male or white counterparts. Schaeffer (2023) states that only 10.6 percent of Fortune 500 firm CEOs are women, and only 4 percent of C-suite leaders are women of color, according to Ellsworth (2022).

I've observed a similar scarcity of women and people of color in senior leader roles in companies where I've worked, and where my coaching clients have worked. In most organizations, the higher up you look on the organizational chart, the less diverse it becomes by gender and race. As you attempt to climb the career ladder as a woman or person of color, you should expect that the higher you climb, the less likely the hiring managers for those roles will look like you. Stated another way, there is a greater chance that white, male hiring managers have more experience hiring other white men, rather than hiring women or people of color. We need those hiring managers to overcome any discomfort or hesitancy they may have about hiring someone unlike anyone they have hired before. A study by Norman et al (2010) showed that a person's positivity impacts perceived trust others have in that person, and the perceived effectiveness of that person. Exuding positivity is a strategic way you can influence the perceived trust the hiring manager has in you, and how they perceive your potential effectiveness.

Let me share an example of a time when I was hired because the hiring manager had more perceived trust in me than in the other finalist because of my positive energy. Long after I had been hired into the role and we had become close, trusted colleagues, my hiring manager told me the story of how things had unfolded during the hiring process. The role being filled was almost exclusively client-facing, and success in the role would require building rapport and trust with clients. While I had more impressive credentials than the other candidate, apparently the other candidate had more direct work experience in the field than I did. The choice should have been an easy one—the other candidate had, on paper, a better proven track record than I did. However, the hiring manager was struggling to make the decision. Why? Because I had built rapport with her far more quickly, and more authentically, than the other candidate had. She told me she found my positive energy uplifting, and it inspired her to believe in me. She asked herself which candidate she would prefer to spend the next few years working with in close collaboration. Since I was apparently far more positive than the other candidate, she preferred me. And because she believed clients would be uplifted, inspired, and have more trust in me than the other candidate, she offered the job to me.

When I speak of exuding positivity, my coaching clients sometimes think that means they should strive to be agreeable and nurturing. Exuding positivity is about being optimistic and confident, regardless of any past failures and setbacks. Whereas being agreeable typically means going along with others and avoiding conflict, even at the expense of voicing your own opinions. Exuding positivity does *not* mean you should strive to agree with others or suppress voicing contrary opinions. That said, when women don't express the gender norms of an agreeable persona, authors like Dorie Clark (2018) state that women are often penalized and labeled in a way men are not. To overcome this, what has worked well for me and my coaching clients is to express our views confidently, even if they are contrary to others, in a respectful and constructive way. The fact is, we should be able to discuss almost anything in the workplace as long as it is done respectfully, while exuding positivity.

What Prevents Positivity?

What if you want to be positive, but find you are mired in the things that drag you down? You don't have enough time to do the things that would make you happy; you don't have enough money to go places that would make you happy; you don't have enough friends or the right kind of friends to be happy; you don't have the car/house/clothes/ stuff that would make you happy; you don't have the time to meditate or workout, although doing those things would make you happy; you don't have the right job title or leader to make you happy … I hope you can snap yourself out of this loop. If you focus solely on what you don't have, you won't be able to reflect on and rejoice in what you *do* have.

Chances are that when you focus on what you don't have, it is because you are comparing yourself to others. That social comparison lowers our happiness according to Arthur Brooks (2022) in his book *From Strength to Strength*. Social media has exacerbated unhappiness because it is so easy to compare yourself/your things to what others allegedly do and have. I'm not questioning the authenticity of their posts. I am suggesting that you ask yourself whether folks on social media are truly happy just because they post that they are doing something "special" or have something "special." How many times have you been in a gorgeous location and seen people who are clearly not present in their surroundings because they are so focused on taking a picture to post? While at the beach, they are so busy posing for the perfect shot that they miss the beauty of the waves, or they miss seeing a dolphin swim past. Are they happy to be on the beach, or are they hoping to be happy by making others envious that they are at the beach? How much of their happiness in that moment depends on how many likes they receive?

If you are waiting for something or someone to make you happy, you're chasing a tenuous target. You can always find someone who has more or a seemingly better fill-in-the-blank (money/car/house/family, etcetera) than you. Comparing yourself to them will most likely make you unhappy. You can also find someone who has less than you, and that comparison might make you happy. In such a case, the only difference between your happiness and unhappiness will be which direction you choose to look.

Tactics to Build Positivity

People who exude positivity have an air of confidence that influences those around them to perceive them as potential stars. How can one generate positivity?

Build Positive Nonverbals and the Mind Will Follow

There are specific nonverbal behaviors that exude positivity, such as open body language. Learn to demonstrate open body language and others will perceive you as positive.

When standing up, open body language includes arms open (not folded), fists relaxed, body facing those you are speaking with, legs approximately hip-width apart and making lasting eye contact (but not staring). When seated, open body language includes arms resting on table or chair arms, but not folded, your face and body should be turned towards the person with whom you're talking, point your feet towards them too (even if they cannot see your feet) and make lasting eye contact without staring. Open body posture signals you are approachable, listening, relaxed, and confident. There is mixed research about whether one needs to smile to be perceived as confident. When working with clients, I recommend you study the nonverbals of senior leaders to gauge whether smiling is the norm. Every single one of the nonverbal behaviors listed above can be practiced and learned. You can absolutely learn to exude positivity!

An additional behavior that influences others' perception of your positivity is how close you stand or sit to them while you communicate. A good rule of thumb is to be within three feet of the person. Any closer and you invade their personal bubble. Any further apart, and you will be perceived as unapproachable and aloof.

One final note is that using open body postures even influences your own mind in a positive way. If you ever feel uncertain or insecure, move your body into a more open body posture and it will change how you feel.

Seek a Regular Practice

Throughout my career, as I examined research studies and observed people to learn more about how positivity is built and expressed, one common theme I found was that positive individuals spend a lot of time in introspection. While that introspection may have many different names, such as prayer, meditation, journaling, coaching, or therapy, positive folks have a regular practice and follow it consistently.

In my search for the keys to positivity, I have spent innumerable hours learning about happiness, Buddhism, indigenous wisdom, reiki, and mindfulness. There are some amazing guides and authors out there, such as Eckhart Tolle, Louise Hay, Marty Seligman, Jamie Sams, Ellen Langer, and Daniel Gilbert, to name a few. When initially working to enhance my own mindful positivity, I couldn't fully understand all the concepts I read. But as I continued learning from those authors and guides by reading their books, I realized that by practicing introspection; I began to *recognize* those exact experiences and encounters that help us learn specific concepts at the right time.

Positive people use their practice and introspection to clearly state their goals, and request what they need to achieve those goals. Some call this prayer; others call it manifestation. In my experience, the more clearly we articulate what it is we want, and what we want to work on, resources and people show up in our lives to help make those things happen. It has worked in my life, and it has worked with my coaching clients. If you are vague about what you want, the universe cannot deliver. However, when we are clear about what we want and need, we will receive the very resources and support we need at specific times in our life and career from God/the angels/the universe (whatever you believe in). For example, something inspired you to pick up this book at this specific time in your career. Pay attention to the specific parts of the book that are resonating deeply with you.

During times of introspection throughout my career, I realized the more grateful I was, the more things I experienced for which to be grateful. Gratitude begot greater gratitude. Joy begot greater joy. Simple things like being generous with my expressions of recognition, whether it be a smile, a hug, a card, or a verbal thank you are always so well received and lift the recipients, and in doing so make me grateful and ever more positive. As I express joy and gratitude, it builds up the joy of those around me. As long as you are authentically grateful and authentically joyful, if you express that gratitude and joy, it will lift everyone around you. Make gratitude a consistent part of your chosen practice. Here are two well-known ways to embed gratitude into your life:

- Begin and end each day by listing people and things for which you are grateful.

- It is impossible to be grumpy and grateful simulta-neously. If you find yourself brooding about what is wrong with your life/career, force yourself to list the things for which you are grateful in your life/career.

One of my coaching clients struggled with this exercise. She would list something positive, then add a "but" to the sentence. I would make her start the verbal exercise over, without using the word "but." She struggled so much that I made it part of her coaching assignments to document in her journal. With practice, it became much easier for her to express and project gratitude.

Find the practice that best aligns with your values and beliefs. Be patient with yourself. It is unlikely you'll be able to enhance your positivity overnight, especially if you have become accustomed to focusing on what you don't have and on what is wrong. But if you consistently work on developing this new daily habit of being grateful and stick with it, you will begin to exude positivity. Keep practicing that until it becomes second nature. Others will feel and see your positive energy and be drawn to you.

Cultivate Your Listening Skills

Why does the ability to listen deeply and truly hear others help with your positivity? It helps for two reasons. One reason is that hearing others' stories gives you a new perspective on your own experiences. Not everyone's experience will be worse than yours, but maybe you'll find that things you struggle with are not just unique to you but something others also have to deal with. You'll be able to shake things off more easily if you realize it's fairly normal to experience the problems you're experiencing.

I recall an experience during my doctoral program when I ran into a classmate as he was heading to the graduate school's administration office. He told me he was going to drop out of the program because he was struggling to keep his head above water in the advanced statistics courses. I was shocked. When I told him I felt exactly the same way about those courses, he couldn't believe it because apparently, I never showed or voiced frustration while in class. He and I sat right down there on the steps and chatted for about an hour, at the end of which he decided things weren't as dire as they seemed. While his situation had not changed, he now knew he was not alone. After that day, he and I would commiserate any time things felt particularly hairy. And that classmate successfully completed the doctoral program with me!

A second reason to sharpen your deep listening skills is because it creates a positive connection with others, which is mutually uplifting. Deep listening means you stay focused on what the other person is saying instead of focusing on your reply. It means not tuning out what they are saying. Deep listening allows you to hear what matters to someone, what they value, and sometimes even what their values are. Think of how it feels when you have told someone about your family (just for the sake of this example), and at a later time they ask about your family members by name. Compare that to how it feels when you are asked questions about your family when you have already shared that information with that person in the past.

When I was in healthcare, I would work with teams to help them learn to truly listen to patients, especially when the patients were unhappy. My instruction to each team was simple: Do *not* interrupt the patient; when they stop talking, based on what you heard, repeat their main concerns back to them. They are simple instructions but very hard to implement without practice and being intentional. This simple approach works wonders to make patients feel heard and validated. And the approach works for all situations. When we allow others to speak without interrupting them, and we validate what we have heard them say, it makes them feel heard, and gives them a positive impression of us and the interaction.

I love observing people during networking events. So many folks practice the opposite of deep listening during such events. At those events, something I really hate is when I am speaking with someone, but they keep looking over my shoulder to see if there is anyone more important that they should meet. That behavior creates such a negative impression! These folks seem to think what matters is the number of names and contact details they collect, or the number of folks with a prominent role they meet. What I don't see are signs of them actually trying to have a real conversation (with deep listening) with anyone. What meaningful thing(s) do you recall about anyone you met at a networking event? And how many of the folks you meet at a networking event will remember something meaningful about you? If you meet those folks again at a future event, will you be able to ask them something pertinent to what they shared with you at your previous meeting? Practice deep listening, and you will find yourself making positive connections with others and it'll create a positive perception of you in their minds, too.

The Art of a Quick Recovery

Now is a good time to talk about recovery rates. People who exude positivity don't have freakishly perfect lives. What they do have is a great recovery rate, and the ability to make sense of and assign value even to those things that have been less than ideal in their lives. When a positive person experiences something negative in their lives, it may throw them for a loop and knock them down for a little while. But their recovery rate, their ability to dust themselves off and get moving again in the right direction, is rapid.

Most positive people I know have learned the art of a quick recovery. I believe it is because they can assign value, i.e. something good, even to the negative experiences. They don't get stuck thinking that things will never get better. They are optimistic that things will get better, and perhaps that's because they have changed the way they think about the negative experience. They learn to change the situation. Positive people believe something good happened in spite of or perhaps because of a negative experience. And as a result, they don't get bogged down by dwelling on that negative experience. They look at what is now better and move forward.

Positive people also don't get bogged down by fearing that something could go wrong because they know if something does go wrong, they have the self-confidence to get through it. Positive people excel at being present.

They focus on experiences as they are occurring without worrying about the future or staying embroiled in the past. It reminds me of a great story I once read about two monks on a walking trek. On their trek, the monks came across a fast-flowing river without a bridge. They carefully navigated a path through the water and arrived at the other bank. On that bank, an old lady asked if they could help her cross the river. Since there were no boats, one of the monks hoisted the old lady on his back and carefully took her to the other side. He rejoined the second monk, and they continued their journey. Many miles later, the second monk said to the first, "I cannot believe you carried that woman across the river. Our practice does not allow us to touch women." The first monk replied, "I only carried her the short distance across the river. You have been carrying her for all these miles since we left the river." Do you have any experience that is keeping you embroiled in the past?

I recall a time when I was on a gorgeous beach in Florida. While walking quietly on the sand, I encountered a woman who struck up a conversation with me. She asked whether I was traveling alone and mentioned that it was her first time doing so as she had been stood up by a friend. I shared that I had had many amazing solo trips and experiences, and hoped she would love her first solo trip. She launched into a depressing monologue about how her life had turned out so differently than she expected, and how she had suffered through a long and bitter divorce that left her emotionally, physically, and financially devastated. I listened for a while and then said I hoped that the gorgeous beach and environment were doing wonders to restore her soul. She just kept on with the same depressing monologue. After a while, feeling the waves of negativity pouring off her, and working actively not to become depressed myself, I asked how long ago the divorce had taken place. Her answer astounded me—it had happened eight years prior! Eight years! And here she was telling a total stranger about it as though it had happened mere months earlier. I signaled a waiter and paid him to deliver a large margarita to her, wished her well in letting go of past hurts and wished her joy in being able to experience the majesty God/the angels/the universe (whatever you believe) had created for us on that beach. And then I continued on with my walk, giving thanks for a tangible lesson on what happens when we don't let go of negativity and resentment.

A simple but effective way I often use to help my coaching clients snap themselves out of brooding on past negative experiences is to get them to first acknowledge how much time and energy they're wasting while they worry about what's happened in the past that they cannot change. The client is asked to find a tangible way to track every single time they think of the negative experience during a specific timeframe. For example, during the course of a week, they put a penny in a jar each time they think about the negative experience. At the end of the week, seeing all the pennies can be a visceral wake up call for the client to think about what productive things they could do with their time instead.

Reflection Questions for Exuding Positivity

Exuding positivity means that no matter the reality you are facing, you continue to have a positive, optimistic perspective of how things will work out. People who exude positivity convey confidence and a can-do quality. Others perceive them to be approachable and effective.

- What is your regular mindful or spiritual practice? Is there anything you need to do to carve out time for that practice more consistently? What will you commit to doing for yourself?

- Find a video of yourself making a presentation (or make a new video of yourself if you don't have one). Carefully critique your nonverbal body language and, if needed, develop a plan to better align your nonverbal language with your intentions.

- Think of specific instances during your career when you faced a major challenge or a roadblock. Describe your recovery rate and evaluate yourself based on several incidents that come to mind. What might you do, specifically, to speed up your recovery rate in the future?

Chapter Three

Honing Your Competencies

Highly successful professionals know themselves well. They know what matters most to them; they know their strengths and weaknesses; they know their triggers; and they know their potential derailers. Most importantly, they continuously work on their personal development to overcome the things that could detract from their positive impact. If you have not been working on your personal development, it is never too late to start. No matter where you are in your career, start now!

As a woman or a person of color, knowing your vulnerabilities allows you to anticipate problems that may come up. Develop an awareness of those who may disregard your opinion, dismiss you, and discount your work. This allows you to develop a plan and ways to work on overcoming those vulnerabilities. You will be held to a different, and at times, higher standard than others. While I certainly perceived this to be the case in my career, and from observations of my clients' careers, data validates our perceptions to be a reality. As a woman your judgement is 1.5 times more likely to be questioned, others are 1.5 times more likely to get credit for *your* ideas, and others are two times more likely to comment on your emotional state (McKinsey & Company, 2023). Knowing this fact, enhancing your competencies to make yourself an expert, and developing a reputation for being *the* expert in your workplace, reduces the probability that your judgement will be questioned or that others may get credit for your ideas.

There are two kinds of competencies you may need to develop to be highly successful: technical competencies and broader career-enhancing competencies. Technical competencies are the skills and knowledge of proficient experts in your career field. Enhancing your technical competencies may involve attaining certifications, licensure, or formal education to establish your technical expertise. It is important that others are made aware of your technical expertise, which is why you should include relevant credentials on your signature line for outgoing emails, and consider displaying diplomas in your workspace, especially if the diploma-granting institution has name recognition and cachet.

What falls under the scope of broader career-enhancing competencies? These include communication skills, negotiation skills, an ability to build rapport and trust, and the skills and knowledge to influence others. As stated earlier, while results get you noticed early in your career, specific behaviors keep you visible as a candidate for advancement opportunities and promotions the rest of your career. Should you want to enhance behavioral competencies, start by identifying the specific behaviors recognized and rewarded in your company, then develop a plan to emulate those behaviors.

The literature is clear that when people are asked to describe ideal leadership qualities, the traits they list tend to be associated with the masculine stereotype. Armed with this knowledge, your personal development focus should be to squash any specific behaviors and communication aspects that detract from your credibility and perceived potential for advancement. I'm not suggesting you adopt behaviors contrary to your values—in fact, I have dedicated a whole chapter to the topic of authenticity. What I am suggesting is that you examine and assess how all your current behaviors enhance or detract from your credibility. Use past feedback from performance reviews and mentors to help with this task. One very specific behavior I highly recommend you consider adopting, is to act like you belong. When you find yourself in new professional environments in which you have never been, when you are (finally) invited to join highly selective meetings, tamp down any imposter syndrome that may surface and act like you belong. What will that entail? Don't exhibit nervousness and observe and mirror what others are doing.

Your Personal Development Goal(s)

What is your goal for your personal development? Which competencies (technical or broader) do you want to enhance and why? Are you able to clearly articulate your short- and long-term goals, as well as the various ways you plan to achieve those goals? If you cannot articulate your goals, or which competencies you want to develop, others won't be able to advocate for you or pave the way for you to achieve them.

How do you determine what matters most to you? How do you learn about your strengths, weaknesses, triggers, and derailers? A common way to learn about some of these things is through assessments such as a 360 review, Hogan assessment, or DiSC assessment. But in my experience, most folks file away the results from these types of one-off assessments rather than figuring out how to embed those learnings into their ongoing personal development. In other words, many don't see the value of applying what they learn from doing the one-off assessments to elevate and increase their opportunities. They check the box on completing the assessment instead of leveraging the results to further their own growth trajectory. You cannot expect your manager or your company to prioritize your development. You are the key to optimizing your own personal and professional development. Take the reins and take control.

Here is an example of what I am talking about. I once had a direct report, let's call her Alice, who transferred in to join my team and complained that the company had not invested in her development since she joined the company several years prior. Hearing that, I told her we would make that topic a priority for each of our bi-weekly touchpoints. I started each touchpoint by asking Alice about her goals and objectives for development, and paths she had researched to achieve those goals so that I could be her advocate for company funding. Each time I asked, she would launch into complaints about the past rather than answering the question. I would redirect her and tell her she needed to come to the next touchpoint with goals/objectives and possible paths. For weeks, she would tell me she didn't have time to complete the assignment, and each time I would tell her I couldn't advocate for her development if I didn't know what exactly she wanted to do. Finally, she gave me a goal as well as a specific certification program she wanted to pursue. In response, I advocated for the company to pay for her certification and got approval. I informed Alice she had the green light and told her to register for the program right away.

During subsequent touchpoints, I asked when the program would begin, and Alice would tell me she hadn't yet registered. And each time I would tell her to do so right away, since doing so would guarantee the company would cover the costs through its completion, but if she did not and financial circumstances changed, there might not be such a guarantee. Four months after I had secured approval for Alice's certification program, and after a particularly tough financial quarter for the company, a mandate was issued that any non-essential expense requests had to get the company CFO's approval. Sadly, Alice still had not registered by that time, and my leader shelved approval for her certification program. By the time the mandate was lifted, my role had been expanded, and I was no longer Alice's leader and was no longer able to advocate for her development. Alice left the company two years later, without that certificate.

When I'm approached by potential coaching clients, at times they are vague about why they want to work with a leadership coach. They may tell me they want to "be more successful" or "be better" without being able to define what that means to them. Asking a potential client to outline their goals for our coaching relationship gives me a good sense of how well we will work together as coach and client. Are they willing to do the hard work to outline what they want to work on, and why they need a coach for that journey?

If you want to have meaningful, productive time in a coaching relationship, you must have clarity about your goals. Without a goal, how will your coach know the kind of support and guidance to provide? Without a goal, how will you be able to ascertain whether time with your coach was a good use of your time and money? If you are struggling to define your goals, here are some suggestions about how to get started:

- There is a huge amount of research published (written and audio) on the topic of leadership success. Even if you do not strive to lead others, the same competencies that tap folks for leadership excellence may allow you to excel on your professional journey. Spend time learning what others have written and posted on this topic.

- Sign up for classes and conferences, especially those for and by women and people of color. Learn how other women and people of color achieved their success. What goals did they set, and how did they achieve them?

- Do a deep dive into any assessments you have had done at different points in your career. What areas did those assessments say you needed to develop and better manage?

Spend the necessary time to articulate what matters most to you, and to identify goals and competencies you need to develop.

Personal Retreats to Renew Your Competency Goals

One way to determine what matters most is to carve out time for personal retreats to determine what is going well with your career, what you are struggling with, and what you need to change to increase your success. When I worked full time in corporate America, I used to take regular personal retreats for this purpose. I would travel somewhere by myself and journal about the things I was processing and then I would use that journal to guide my development efforts when I returned to work.

Many friends and acquaintances would express jealousy at my ability to take those personal retreats. But as I told them, what matters is making the commitment to yourself and your own development, not that you take a trip to some faraway place. It is the process of making a commitment to yourself that is powerful, no matter how you realize that commitment! Whether you commit to one hour a month for yourself or five, whether you use that time for self-development in a coffee shop, while you work out, or even while you commute, what matters is that you follow through on your commitment to yourself. And for those who tell me they cannot carve out one hour a month for themselves, I ask why other people and tasks take a higher priority than themselves? Start small—even twenty minutes for the first month—schedule that time on your calendar, turn off all distractions (phone/TV/email) and work through these questions:

- What is going well with your career?

- What are you struggling with?

- What do you need to start doing, stop doing, or continue to do to enhance what is going well, and overcome challenges?

You may have to research solutions to help you, but consider that research time an investment in yourself, and a further commitment to your professional success.

If you are able to physically distance yourself from your regular environment for your personal retreats, studies show there are significant cognitive benefits to being in nature. Read up on forest bathing and cognitive sciences for more about this topic. There is something indescribably powerful about being surrounded by nature's majestic beauty, sitting in silence with your own thoughts and feelings, and being able to deeply reflect on your professional progress.

On my personal retreats, some of the most profound revelations have come to me while on trips to places like Canada's Banff National Park and game parks in Zambia. In Banff National Park, the scale of the incredible mountains and vistas is hard for the brain to comprehend. I was struck by how tiny we humans are in comparison to the mountains, and how insignificant the human lifespan is compared to that of the mountains. If you have had the fortune to go on safari in Africa, you can relate to the wondrous awe of being among wild animals in their element. Seeing the size and power of majestic elephants, juxtaposed with how gentle they can be is deeply moving. It is hard to articulate the feelings that bubble up in me when I am on a game drive in Zambia. Time slows down, and I feel recalibrated with each safari experience. It is a humbling and deeply grounding experience that touches my soul. Being in the presence of natural majesty, whether among the mountains or on the plains of Africa, helps me temper any professional or personal problems I am facing.

Find the places where you can be grounded on your personal retreats. It does not have to be an expensive or exotic location (recall that Zambia is not an exotic location for me; it is home), but it must be someplace where you can think and reflect deeply without interruptions.

Refine Your Competencies Through a Commitment to Learning

Early in my career, I read the occasional professional book or article, but it was not something I did on a regular basis. I also rarely *did* anything with what I read. I was studying, but I was not learning—I wasn't taking the time to apply and integrate what I had studied into my daily professional life. It wasn't until later in my career that I grasped I had to integrate and apply what I was studying and, thus, demonstrate my learnings. For example, it wasn't until my job required me to make regular presentations to audiences of various sizes that I saw how invaluable it was to study how others framed concepts, how they used creative examples or drew insightful conclusions. I began focusing my studies on leadership development and happiness/mindfulness spaces, and made the commitment to apply what I was studying. The more I read and listened to podcasts and the more I integrated those learnings into my practice, the more I succeeded. My presentations were better received by audiences, my evaluations from peers and leaders became exemplary, and I received more recognition and promotions. There was a direct correlation between my learning and my success.

How much of a commitment have you made to your own learning and development? Do you subscribe to trade journals and industry newsfeeds? Are you a member of industry associations that have regular speakers and content sharing? Are you working on enhancing your formal education? And most importantly, how exactly are you integrating all your learnings into your regular practice? One simple technique is to focus on integrating or practicing one idea a month, or perhaps a quarter. Find the cadence that works to keep you motivated but not overwhelmed. Post the idea somewhere visible or even on your calendar as a reminder for your chosen duration of a month or quarter. I recommend keeping a journal to track what you are working on, and regularly assess how well you are incorporating those ideas into your practice. At the end of the year, evaluate how well you've integrated all the ideas you learned and incorporated into your work during that year.

For those who need a gentle nudge with accountability, this is a great example of the kind of work you can do with a leadership coach. You can even work with your coach to lead you through a curated "study guide" of topics, articles, and books. Other ways to have structured and group learning is to join professional book clubs or sign up for courses and certification programs. However you do it, make sure you integrate what you have learned into your professional practice and personal development.

Sharpening Your Negotiation Skills

We are all aware of the fact that women do not get paid as equitably as men. The gender pay gap widens as women advance in their careers, meaning as they climb the leadership ladder, women successively make less than their male peers climbing at the same rate (Frank, 2015). A contributing factor is that women negotiate four times less often than men, and when they do negotiate, they ask for less than men (Babcock & Laschever, 2021). We, as women, potentially are contributing to our own problem.

Competency with negotiation skills is a requirement for you to achieve what you are truly worth. Women and people of color who don't have mentors or role models to demonstrate and teach negotiation prowess have a deficit when they join the workforce, and that deficit will grow exponentially if they don't quickly learn to determine what they are worth and negotiate to see it reflected in their earnings. When I first entered the workforce, I had no female role models to advise me on how to negotiate, so I had to learn things the hard way by making mistakes. The good news is that those mistakes soon became visible to me as I compared myself to male peers. I set about educating myself about how to establish the market value of my profession. The bigger challenge was developing the courage to ask for what I was worth. Back then, my fear was that I might lose the promotion or job offer if I negotiated. Later, as I got wiser, I realized a greater fear *should* be getting stuck in a job where I'd successively lose more money during my career if I didn't negotiate for what I was worth. I finally understood that even if I moved to a different firm, if I had not negotiated well with the first firm, it could potentially have a detrimental impact on my next compensation package because I would be negotiating from a lower threshold starting point.

From the moment I realized how important it was for me to negotiate my compensation package, with each successive negotiation I undertook, the calmer and more factual I was during the negotiation process. I stayed calm knowing I could and would walk away if they did not meet my financial range. I took a stand to only accept what I was worth, armed with factual data from performance reviews and verbal assessments from leaders. With each subsequent negotiation, I always got so much more than was initially offered because I asked. Because I asked! Some women are getting paid less than their male peers because they are willing to accept that lower pay grade. You must learn the art of negotiation if you want to succeed professionally.

There are some specific actions you can take to enhance your negotiation skills. The first is to become proficient at mining data to determine your worth. Your source of compensation data should include sources internal, as well as external, to your current employer. Internally, the compensation department is usually willing to share salary (and total compensation) ranges by title or grade. Use your tenure and your performance evaluations to have discussions with your leader about where and why you are at a specific spot in your pay range, how you compare to peers, and what it will take to progress within your range, or up to the next range. Externally, use online research to find out what the market rate is for your job title, in your region of the country. Once you have determined what your compensation package should look like, use that data in your negotiations.

I advise clients to also look beyond the compensation package for negotiation items. This is one area where having a mentor within the firm will help tremendously. That mentor will be able to tell you which items, besides compensation, the firm is willing to negotiate. Such items may include title, grade, paid time off, flexible schedule, remote work, amount of travel, etc. If you don't have a mentor within your firm, try to get a hold of your HR handbook where such things are outlined.

A second action you can undertake to enhance your negotiation skills is to practice overcoming any potential discomfort during the negotiation process. When I work with clients, I often hear about fear or embarrassment holding them back from negotiating for themselves. I point out to these clients that by not negotiating for themselves, they are stealing what they've lost out on from their children and loved ones. If you feel bad asking for more for yourself, ask for more on behalf of your children and loved ones. Practicing negotiations will help build up your self-confidence and help you convey the right words and attitude during the actual process. Practice with mentors, your coach if you have one, or other seasoned friends and family members. You can also find podcasts and online videos that may help you prepare to negotiate.

Boost Your Competency of Composure by Having a Regular Practice

In an earlier chapter, I spoke about having a regular practice to establish positivity. I also recommend a regular practice to help you bolster the competency of composure. Having a regular practice will enhance your clarity of mind, keep you grounded and focused on what matters most to you, and will help you stay composed. Whether that practice is meditation, prayer, reiki, tai chi, exercise, or some other practice, its goal should be to manage your own thoughts, feelings, and energy. Your practice should help you find a calm, composed state which will be reflected in the energy you project.

From my observations and experience, I've noted that when triggered, people who don't have a regular spiritual practice can quickly spiral out of control with their thoughts and words. Those without a regular practice seem to be more easily triggered by others around them. As a woman or person of color, you are in the minority in the typical workplace. As such, your words and actions will be under greater scrutiny than those in the majority. You don't have the privilege of having a meltdown in the workplace and being able to walk away with your reputation intact. Recall, as a woman, you are two times more likely to hear comments about your emotional state, and more likely to be labeled if you express emotion. As people of color, we can get labeled as angry if we don't stay composed. Having a regular practice will make you less reactive, help you manage feelings as they emerge, and help you temper your words/energy. Stay composed on the outside even if you are getting emotional on the inside. Don't give others reasons to label you or negatively impact your career success.

Reflection Questions for Honing Your Competencies

As a woman or a person of color, you will be held to a different, and at times, higher standard than others. There are two kinds of competencies you need to develop to be perceived as highly successful: technical competencies, and broader career-enhancing competencies.

- What is going well with your career? What are you struggling with?

- Which competencies (technical or broader) do you want to sharpen? How do you plan to enhance them?

- What was the last thing you studied, and how have you integrated that knowledge into your professional life?

_____

_____

_____

_____

_____

_____

_____

_____

_____

_____

_____

_____

_____

_____

_____

_____

_____

_____

_____

_____

_____

_____

_____

_____

_____

Chapter Four

Building a Robust Support System

It is lonely being a woman and a person of color in the professional world. When I first began my career, I didn't see senior leaders who looked like me. I couldn't relate to the tales and experiences of the senior leaders I saw, and as a consequence my professional support system was lacking. However, even in those instances where there were more senior female leaders and leaders of color, I was unprepared for the degree to which these individuals did not or would not provide support to others who looked like them. My experience was not unique—studies show that senior female leaders, unlike their male counterparts, typically do not or will not mentor or assist their female juniors up the ladder.

What this means is that early in my career, I made professional decisions without having the privilege of a sounding board of trusted advisors. And looking back, I understand why the gap grew between those who had advisors and those of us who didn't. Once I had grasped how important it was to have trusted advisors, and realized that I needed to establish that resource in my own professional life, I began actively seeking out suitable candidates for my personal board of directors. The quality of my professional journey improved exponentially as I built and developed my support system. I didn't feel so alone; I had safe places to vent; and I had trusted colleagues who could advise me on how to navigate political and professional minefields. In this chapter, my goal is to make the process of building a robust professional support system more efficient for you than it was for me. The sooner you have your support system, the sooner those members can help you shatter the glass ceiling.

What is my definition of a support system? It is a group of individuals from whom you'll learn lessons so that you can avoid the mistakes they made; it is a group of individuals who give you a trusted place to critique your ideas and plans; it is a group of individuals who create a safe place for you to vent and share any vulnerabilities; and it is a group of individuals who will encourage you and lift you up when you need it. The sooner you have a robust support system, the sooner you can tap them to reinforce and encourage you on your career trajectory. As a woman or person of color, you will be held to a different, and at times, higher standard than others. You need to have as much support as possible to help you navigate such political waters. As a woman or person of color, knowing there may be few who look like you in senior roles where you work, this chapter will lay out what to look for in potential supporters, and where to find folks for your professional support system.

What Makes Someone a Good Bet for Your Professional Support System?

One goal in building your support system should be to find individuals who are knowledgeable about your industry and profession. Not every member of your support system has to have experience with your industry or profession, but at least a few members must have experience and contacts in your field to ensure the support you receive is robust. Other goals in building your support system should be to find individuals who can be trusted to keep things confidential, and to find individuals with whom you have good fit—whose voice you can hear, who share similar experiences/perspectives as you, and who will gently but firmly hold you accountable. Let me expand further on these concepts.

Choosing some individuals who know your industry and profession is vital because they'll understand relevant nuances and norms. You won't have to explain how things are in your industry or profession when you select people who have related knowledge and experience. These are folks who use and understand the same professional jargon as you. What will make them invaluable to you is if they have been in your shoes, or currently are in your shoes, and can commiserate with you. That fact alone, the knowledge that it is *not* just you experiencing what you are experiencing, can greatly reduce your angst about your situation and be a huge source of encouragement. Asking them to share their own professional journey will likely yield some valuable nuggets for you. You may be able to learn how to avoid some of the pitfalls they had to circumvent.

The ability to keep things confidential is crucial among members of your support system, if you are to truly open up and allow yourself to be vulnerable with them. What is the point of having people in your support system if you don't trust them enough to share how you truly feel, or you aren't able to share your anxieties and concerns? While it takes time to build trust, when you are considering someone to potentially become a part of your support system, consciously explore how well they inspire trust in you. As you deepen your relationship, assess how well they have kept what you have shared with them confidential.

Choosing folks whose voice you can hear means they communicate in a style that matches your preferred style—they are as assertive and/or empathetic as you want and need them to be. They are a shoulder to cry on, if that's what you need; or deliver great pep talks, if that's that you need; or are assertive about making you toe the line, if that's what you need. In other words, a robust support system has just the right balance of those who make you feel comfortable enough to feel confident and courageous, and those who make you uncomfortable enough to spur you into action without shutting you down. If you are fortunate, your support system will have the perfect combination of communication styles to match your needs. You may go to different members of your support system for different issues, but what is important is that they are collectively there for you.

Choosing some folks with similar perspectives and experiences as your own should be another consideration for your support system. This is important because there is so much that is understood without having to be said, when you have such similarities. Here are some examples of what I mean:

- Whenever I pass a person of color on the street, in a store, or in the workplace, I make eye contact, nod, and greet them. This may seem insignificant if you're not a person of color. To those of us of color, however, it is a tangible way to demonstrate that we see each other and acknowledge each other because in so many aspects of our lives, we don't get to feel that way. Without saying a word, we know we have some shared understanding due to similar lived experiences.

- When I meet someone who has a name that is unusual in spelling or pronunciation, I make a point of learning how to say and spell their name. A name is such an important part of our identities. When others do not take the time to learn to pronounce our name, or learn to spell our name, it can signal we are not important to them. As someone whose first name gets butchered verbally and in writing, I know how insulting it is to have to repeatedly correct the same person who continues to mispronounce my name over and over again. It's one thing if you don't know how to pronounce my name when we first meet, but if I have to keep correcting you, I take it as a lack of caring. When I've run out of patience, I suggest these folks call me Dr. Mathews or just Doctor instead— surely, they can pronounce that!

- Years ago, while interviewing for a position in another state, I had several phone interviews with the corporate recruiter. In our last call before the in-person interview, I asked the recruiter how I would be received in his state as a woman of color. He paused and then answered by giving me demographic statistics of the state. He clearly had no idea what I was asking.

If these examples resonate with you, we have some shared experiences and perspectives. Once again, not every member of your support system needs to share your experiences and perspectives, but you need enough of them to have a safe place to vent and be understood without having to explain things at length.

A few more factors should be considered when building your support system: whether potential candidates care about you and your success, their ability and willingness to hold you accountable, and their availability. Members of your professional support system need to care about you and your success. I've seen some mentors who seem to be more interested in their own reputation rather than actually caring about helping and supporting the individual being mentored. As you work on building your support system, think consciously about how much each person truly cares about you and your success and how they have demonstrated that care.

One tangible way I assess whether someone cares about me professionally is the extent to which they ask about me, listen, and then remember those details I share about myself. If each time you meet a person, you have to repeat things you have already told them, that is a sign they are either not great listeners, or they don't care enough about you to remember. Either way, that is probably a bad candidate for your support system. Keep them in your professional network, but don't add them to your support system.

Being able to hold you accountable should be another consideration for potential members of your support system. If they are not going to help you take accountability for your own professional growth and success, they shouldn't be considered part of your support system. They too fall into the category of your broader network. For you to have a robust professional support system, at least some of the individuals must be able to hold you accountable for achieving your goals and do so in a supportive and helpful way that does not shut you down.

A person's availability should be another consideration factor. Even if a person meets all the qualities covered above, if they are simply not available to you when you need advice/support, they are not good candidates for your support system. At the same time, you need to have realistic expectations of others' availability. I find it helpful to have a regular cadence of virtual or in-person touchpoints with each member of my support system. The frequency I connect with each person is determined between us. And that cadence varies from person to person, based on what works best for our schedules and needs.

Where to Look for Support System Candidates

An obvious place to start your search would be your existing friends and family members. There are pros and cons to having friends and family members in your professional support system. This group of individuals rate high on the caring scale but may not fare as well regarding industry/professional knowledge and their ability to hold you accountable. Family and friends will also need to overcome their biases in your favor, to be frank with you when needed. You know they like and love you—the question is whether they are able and willing to say what needs to be said, without jeopardizing your relationship.

Comb through your existing professional network for potential candidates for your support system. You are likely to find some folks who have the right experience, but you don't yet have a close relationship. In such cases, set up time to meet with them to get to know more about their communication style and availability and begin to explore whether they might be willing to be a part of your personal board of directors. Before you make the ask of them for such a role, be clear about what it is you expect of them so they can decide whether that is a commitment they can make. Be specific—how often you plan to contact them, via what mode (phone, text, email), etcetera. Also, once you explain your intent to expand your professional support system, ask your existing network whether they have contacts you should meet and get to know.

Joining associations can be a great way to meet potential candidates for your support system. If you use this approach, remember that you will need to be proactive in these groups. Passive membership and event attendance won't cut it. Be proactive about volunteering and taking on leadership roles in those associations. Working with other professionals will give you insights into how well they might be as part of your support system. Be intentional about your search for potential advisors at every event you attend. I recall years ago fortuitously meeting Anna at the registration table of an association event and striking up a conversation with her. In the short time it took us to register and walk into the room to find seats, we had established enough rapport that we chose to sit next to each other during the event and exchanged contact information at the end. Right after I left the event, I put a reminder on my calendar to follow up with Anna and ask to meet again over coffee. When we next met, I discovered that like me, Anna had extensive healthcare experience and like me, was one of the few executive women where she worked. Anna and I spoke the same jargon. We had a deep understanding of healthcare nuances; we shared similar experiences as women in leadership, and we had complementary communication styles. Anna soon became a member of my personal board, and I was on hers too, and years later we remain close friends and advisors to each other. I found this member of my support system at a chance meeting. But it was the intentional outreach (by us both), and mutual intentional investment over time, that has allowed our professional relationship to endure. Be intentional about building your support system.

Another option to identify great candidates for your support system is to sign up for mentor programs within industry associations, and even within your firm. The structure of a mentor program will allow you to get to know your mentor, and based on how well they fit your needs and if they meet the other criteria that have been discussed, the program may yield some potential candidates. Mentor programs can also create a potential pool of supporters from other mentors (or even mentees). Be intentional about tapping such pools as you build your support system.

What you *don't* want to do is sign up for mentor programs for the sole purpose of unearthing advisors—in other words, don't phone it in if you join a mentor program. Do your part to be a fully engaged mentee and participate wholeheartedly in the program. Remember that you are taking up a leader's time, and you are impacting your reputation and credibility through your actions and words. The saying that it is a small world is true—even in large cities, industry professionals who are well-connected talk with each other. Making a poor impression with well-connected professionals will not bode well for your career.

When I work with a mentee, my expectation is that they will set up regular meetings with me, share an agenda of what we will discuss during each meeting, and follow through on any "homework" between meetings. It is not a time for idle chatter and small talk. Instead, I expect the mentee to ask questions about their specific leadership challenges and discuss professional topics they are working on. It has always been important to me to "lift others as I climbed" as the saying goes. I've always been determined *not* to be one of those senior female leaders who won't help others climb the ladder. For this reason, and because I knew how hard the climb was for me, my focus turned to specifically helping other women and people of color where possible.

In one company where I worked, I recall when a woman of color, let's call her Jessica, asked to meet with me. She said she'd heard I was a great mentor who could open doors for others. Jessica asked to become my mentee. I explained my expectations of a mentee, and Jessica agreed. Soon after we began to meet, Jessica became flaky, either not setting up meetings, or showing up without any agenda or topics for discussion. I figured rather than me having to officially terminate the mentorship, if I sat back, she would let it fizzle. And she did. Fast forward a few months and Jessica applied for an internal job and asked me to put in a good word for her. I told her that I couldn't do it based on her behavior. Despite being a strong supporter of women and people of color, I refuse to assist those who don't value excellence, who do shoddy work, or who are lazy. Remember, your actions and words can create a lasting reputation with current and potential members of your support system.

Here is one more helpful avenue to pursue. A leadership coach might be a great addition to round out your support system. While you should have a contractual, collaborative, and confidential relationship with any coach, use some of the same criteria as described above to select the coach who will be most beneficial. In every leadership role I've held, I negotiated for a leadership coach, and if one was not approved, I hired one on my own. My initial criteria is that the coach is a woman of color, or if that is not possible, I choose one who has had a lot of experience coaching women of color. During the initial screening with potential coaches, I look for someone with whom I have rapport, even during that first meeting. I also look for knowledge and experience with my industry, hierarchical stage, complementary communication style, and availability. The higher I rose, the more I relied on my executive leadership coach for support. She was an invaluable key to my success. With her I could safely strategize how to navigate the political environment, safely vent about things that were causing me professional angst, and most importantly, I didn't feel like I was alone.

The Difference Between a Mentor and a Coach

There is a difference between a mentor and a coach. A mentor tends to be someone in the same industry and profession as you, who can share technical knowledge and advice about your industry. A mentoring relationship can vary greatly depending on the mentor, but many mentorships are neither formal nor structured. When I serve as a mentor, the relationship is clearly structured. This is because years ago, I reflected on which of my mentees got the greatest lasting benefit and used that as the blueprint to structure future mentorships. Not all mentors do this. Should you choose to seek out mentors, I recommend you explore the kind of structure that will give you the greatest benefit.

A coaching relationship is one that is confidential, creative, and collaborative. A formal agreement should exist that outlines goals, meeting format and cadence, duration, termination terms, and payment terms. It's possible that the coach you work with won't be in the same industry, but ensure you pick a coach who either has industry expertise or successful experience coaching others in your industry.

The biggest difference between a coach and a mentor is when your mentor is employed in the same firm as you. The mentor will have firsthand knowledge of the internal politics; on the other hand, they are also impacted by those same politics. If you choose a mentor who works at the same firm, be sure to listen to whether they gossip about others or share confidential information about them. If they do so, ask yourself how likely it is that they will keep anything you share with them confidential. Try to gauge the political motivation an internal mentor might have to mentor you. In contrast, when you work with an external coach, you sign a formal agreement ensuring their confidentiality, and their agenda is your success—they aren't tied to internal organizational politics. If you are more successful as a result of the coaching relationship, the coach is more likely to gain future business based on your word of mouth, and even from your firm if that is who hired them for you. Ultimately, nothing prevents you from having mentors, as well as a coach. But it is helpful to know what to expect from each distinct relationship.

Reflection Questions for Building a Robust Support System

It is important for your professional success that you have a robust support system. A support system is a group of individuals from whom you'll learn lessons; it is a group of individuals who give you a trusted place to vet your ideas and plans; it is a group of individuals who create a safe place for you to vent and share vulnerabilities; and it is a group of individuals who will encourage you and lift you up when you need it.

- Make a list of individuals in your support system, indicating for each how often you meet, and what specific kind of support they provide to you. What support gaps exist as you look at the complete list?

- Where will you intentionally seek out candidates to fill any gaps in your support system? Make a list of the steps you will take and set goals for each one.

- On your support system list, are there any members with whom you would benefit from a deeper professional relationship? If so, what are some specific ways in which you could request and plan more time with these individuals? Add a reminder on your calendar to reach out to them once you have considered the best way forward.

_____

_____

_____

_____

_____

_____

_____

_____

_____

_____

_____

_____

_____

_____

_____

_____

_____

_____

_____

_____

_____

_____

_____

_____

Chapter Five

Establishing and Maintaining Boundaries

Establishing boundaries means ensuring your words and behaviors protect and affirm what matters most to you. Ensuring others respect your boundaries means honoring your own needs and advises others how to respect and honor them too. It means speaking up, or behaving in a way that shows others what you will or will not tolerate as acceptable behavior from those around you. The process of maintaining boundaries acknowledges that it typically will require ongoing effort to sustain those boundaries with others over time. The behavior you will get from others is the behavior you accept! Or said another way, others will treat you the way you allow yourself to be treated.

Many of my coaching clients who are women or people of color share stories about their ideas repeatedly being dismissed or shut down in the workplace. The phenomenon is not unique to my clients—as cited earlier, a McKinsey (2023) study found women are 1.5 times more likely to have their ideas questioned and dismissed in the workplace. As I work with my clients, I ask specific questions about the scenarios they describe: what are they are doing and saying as the situation unfolds; what are others doing and saying as the scenario unfolds? In virtually every case, the client did or said something that allowed others to think they were treating my client in an acceptable manner; or the client did *not* do anything or say anything to make others think they were treating my client unacceptably. These are powerful exercises to help my clients see that their own words and behavior, or lack of words and behavior, is allowing others to treat them in certain ways. If you feel you are being treated differently or being held to a higher standard than others and it is unacceptable, analyze whether your words and actions or lack of words and actions signal things are okay, just as they are. Analyze whether your words and actions clearly signal the current situation is unacceptable.

I find that clients who express resentment about others taking advantage of them tend to allow themselves to be taken advantage of repeatedly. I find that clients who express anger at not being treated with the same respect as peers allow themselves to be spoken to far more disrespectfully than their peers. I find clients who don't speak up when they notice inequities for fear of losing their jobs, continue being treated inequitably and, at times, lose their job anyway because no one (including themselves) is advocating for them.

In my experience, the main reason my coaching clients have trouble establishing boundaries with others is out of fear. This ranges from a fear of what may happen if they speak up, to a fear of losing friendships, a fear of not being liked, or a fear of missing out ... the list goes on and on. The problem is that by allowing fear to temper their own needs, they are relinquishing their power to others. The client's behavior itself gives others license to take advantage of them, if they are so inclined.

The minute you feel powerless and trapped professionally, it will negatively impact your ability to establish boundaries. The mindset of feeling powerless will manifest in your behavior, actions, and words into that of passive acquiescence. And eventually, it becomes a cyclical loop: you will keep getting the behavior you accepted in the past from others, until you do something different.

The more you practice small acts of courage to establish boundaries, the more courage you will develop. It is this exact practice that helped me become increasingly courageous throughout my own career. Specifically, I learned a few great, and simple, techniques to use when I found myself in a situation that challenged my boundaries. Here are some of those techniques:

- When someone interrupts you, politely hold up a hand and say something like "Let me finish what I have to say, and then I'll call on you." If they continue to interrupt you, become more assertive and say something like, "I am not done yet."

- When someone says something demeaning, pause the conversation by saying "I know you meant well but that made me feel bad." Or something like "Ouch, that didn't feel good!"

- When someone says or does something demeaning, ask them to clarify exactly what they meant by that statement or action.

- If you are too upset to address an issue when it occurs, or you need time to collect your thoughts, walk away in the moment, but address the issue with that individual later, using one of the techniques above.

I promise, the more you practice, the easier it will get. And it works! I can attest to this in my own life, as well as in hearing about the positive changes in the lives of my clients. Find ways to give yourself a pep talk and put things in perspective. The less you view something as a huge risk professionally, the less you will fear addressing it. The more you practice taking a stand, speaking out, and behaving in ways to establish your boundaries, the more each successive triumph will make the next time that much easier.

As I've shared earlier, when I encounter fear professionally, I tell myself, *unlike skydiving, this is not a life-or-death situation. It is not the end of the world. You can do this.* At times, my clients imply it is easier for me to speak up because I'm more courageous than them. I point out I was not always as courageous as I am now in this phase of life. It has taken a lot of practice to develop the courage they now witness in me. Each time I spoke up or took a stand and was able to successfully transform how others treated me, it fueled my resolve to continue to speak up or take a stand in the future. Practicing courage produced more courage. It begins with practice.

I'll share one early example of something that helped develop the skill to establish boundaries. This example is from my doctoral experience. Getting my PhD was the hardest thing I have ever done but is also one of the most meaningful investments I have ever made in myself. The final phase of the PhD process is the successful completion of a dissertation. The doctoral student works with a PhD committee throughout the entire dissertation process. The very last step is for that committee to approve the written dissertation, as well as oral defense, once they feel it merits approval. In other words, a doctoral student cannot complete their PhD without the explicit approval of their committee. The chair of the committee is a crucial member and part of the student's success. That individual helps to select the right committee members and ensure politics within the committee don't cause slowdowns or breakdowns in the process. The chair is also the person with whom the doctoral student works most closely.

For these reasons, I asked my doctoral advisor, with whom I had worked with for years and respected deeply, to be the chair of my dissertation committee. My advisor asked me to include a specific faculty member, let's call him Dr. Martin, as the co-chair. I didn't have a close working relationship with Dr. Martin, and didn't love his communication style, so I was not enamored with the suggestion of making him co-chair. However, with the assurance of my advisor that Dr. Martin was a good choice, I acquiesced. I am intentionally using the word acquiesce in that sentence. I wanted my advisor to lead the committee and if that was conditional on "letting him" have Dr. Martin as co-chair, I was willing to go along with it. If I had had the power to truly choose my committee, Dr. Martin would not have been on the committee, let alone been a co-chair.

Relatively early in the dissertation period, I had a formal and public presentation to defend my dissertation proposal. As my advisor introduced me to the crowd before my presentation, he made an announcement that due to the expansion of his faculty role to dean, he would remain on my dissertation committee but would hand over the committee chair reins to Dr. Martin. I was shocked and horrified about the decision, but mostly I could not believe he was making the announcement literally minutes before I had to make a very crucial presentation! Somehow, I got through the presentation and had no choice but to begin working closely with Dr. Martin as my committee chair. I felt powerless about the entire thing.

It would take me two more years to complete the dissertation, while working full-time. I found it incredibly difficult working with Dr. Martin. His style of communication simply did not complement my learning style. I learn best when I understand why something is the way it is. I like seeing data/analysis that leads my logical brain to reach the same conclusions as the person making a particular point. Dr. Martin's communication style was to state a point of view and expect me to go along with it, without sharing any of the data/analysis supporting that view. He may have interpreted my questions as an effort to challenge him, but actually, I was just trying to understand why one way was better than another.

To get the PhD, I had to get Dr. Martin's approval. Over those two years, everything felt like a battle reinforcing how powerless I was. Two examples that stand out are (1) when Dr. Martin removed someone that I respected and liked from the committee without my consent, and (2) during the final stages of the process, as Dr. Martin and I were engaged in yet another heated debate, he stated if I wanted to get the PhD; I needed to stop arguing and just do what he was telling me to do! In the end, because I had no choice and was powerless, I did as I was told and was finally able to successfully complete the PhD.

This prolonged and painful dissertation period made me vow never to allow anyone to have that kind of power over me professionally, ever again. The dissertation process helped me learn what it is like to be powerless without being able to establish any boundaries. That process helped me develop the strength to put boundaries in place for the rest of my career. Specifically, I vowed to have the courage to speak up when things were not in my best interest or violated my values. Interestingly, learning how to better set boundaries is an area where I do a considerable amount of work with my coaching clients.

Think about any professional experiences you have had where you felt powerless. What did you do or say in that moment? Do you have any regrets about not doing or saying anything in that scenario? Imagine yourself as a superhero with all the skills and knowledge to handle people and situations perfectly. Armed with those skills and knowledge, what would you have done or said differently when that happened? Make notes about your thoughts and how you would handle a similar situation differently today and find a way to integrate doing so into your ongoing development.

No matter how you develop the skill of setting boundaries, learning and implementing these skills is a process you need to work through to excel in your career. When you know what matters to you, are you able to say no to things that won't honor those needs? When you know being around certain individuals drains you, do you honor your own energy and limit the amount of time you spend with those people? If you are unable to say no to these situations or people, I encourage you to learn to elevate your needs over the needs of those to whom you are acquiescing. What keeps you from saying no? Why are you giving away your power?

Learn How to Respectfully Maintain Your Boundaries

Setting boundaries and having the power to say no does not mean you have to be a bully, be mean, or even be loud. However, the way in which you speak up to establish boundaries should match the culture of the organization in which you work. If you assert yourself aggressively and your organization's culture does not value that, you will be labeled a bully, and it may work against you. If you assert your boundaries far more gently than your peers and organizational culture value, you may find others ignoring or overriding you. If you find that you are not getting what you want, if you feel that others are taking advantage of you, reflect deeply on whether that is because you are not enforcing your boundaries, or because you are not doing so in a way that matches your organizational culture.

One of my leaders used to say that I had a powerful presence without having to use a hammer. I love that expression. Being treated with respect matters a lot to me, so it is a courtesy I extend to others. Just because I must assert a boundary does not mean I have to be disrespectful to others as I do so.

The first time I practiced setting a boundary, respectfully, was early in my career. I was tapped to lead a high-profile, company-wide committee to select a new vendor for a key service. It required that I convene a committee and facilitate regular meetings for more than thirty key leaders from across the company. When it was time for vendor presentations, scheduling time slots when all thirty could attend was a virtual impossibility, so instead I picked time slots when the vast majority of the committee was available.

Soon after I had scheduled the vendor presentations, I received a call from a senior vice president whom we shall call Cindy. She outranked me by at least four hierarchical levels. Cindy was upset because none of her four team members would be able to attend one of the three scheduled vendor presentations. When I answered the phone, Cindy began berating me, yelling about how disrespectful it was of me to exclude her team, etc., etc. She yelled so loudly over the phone that peers in my office suite could hear her! I literally could not get a word in to explain before Cindy hung up on me.

I was badly shaken after the phone call. I was angry about being yelled at so rudely. I was angry that Cindy assumed I hadn't done extensive work to include as many committee members as possible for every vendor presentation; and I was angry that she didn't want to hear what I had to say. She just wanted me to fix it for her team, regardless of what that might mean for others on the committee. I knew I had to confront Cindy about her phone call, but I also knew I was too angry to think clearly. Cindy's bad behavior was a reflection on her, not on me. But if I had confronted her immediately after she hung up on me, I knew it would be hard for me to be respectful. She needed to be called out, respectfully, for her bad behavior.

It is my belief that we should be able to discuss almost anything in the workplace as long as it is done respectfully. For this reason, I decided I would go to see Cindy the next day because she had overstepped my boundary of treating me with respect. I prayed hard and rehearsed what I would say, but it was still nerve-wracking to confront a senior vice president.

The next day, I went to Cindy's office without an appointment. I knocked on her door. When she opened it, I said, "Thank you for calling me yesterday to give me an opportunity to solve this scheduling problem for your team. I'm currently looking for a new time slot with that vendor." Cindy appeared flustered and began to apologize for getting so upset on the phone. I simply nodded my head, and left her office. I was not going to let her think a simple apology made everything okay, and I was not going to waste any of my time trying to make her feel better. But by nodding, I acknowledged that she had apologized. Cindy was never rude to me again for the rest of the time we worked together. It was a defining successful moment in my career. You will get from others the behavior you accept!

There are other aspects of the encounter with Cindy that were learning experiences for me. As a result, I have developed a series of tactics I share with coaching clients. First is that I stayed calm while the horrid phone call was taking place. In an earlier chapter, I shared the art of a quick recovery. Staying calm on that call was an example of a quick recovery. Cindy called me out of the blue. Her call was unexpected, and her tone and yelling were unbelievable. I could feel myself getting angry, so I focused on not saying anything I might regret later. Since Cindy didn't allow me to speak on that call, holding back what I wanted to say was an unnecessary effort on my part. But in other professional encounters in my career, I have learned not to show others a visible or emotional reaction, especially when emotions are bubbling within me. Remember, studies show women are often penalized and labeled in a way men are not. I refuse to give others ammunition, through my own words/actions, to attack and label me.

Second, I took the time to calm down overnight and collect my thoughts about what to say, before I confronted Cindy the next day. Be intentional about the words you use when you are establishing boundaries with others. Since being treated with respect and treating others with respect is one of my values, I worked hard to find just the right words to be direct but respectful with Cindy. And once I found the right words, I practiced saying them with just the right energy to clearly deliver the message with just the right punch. You may wonder what I did to calm myself down after that phone call and that evening when I got home. I used the things I do in my regular practice (also covered in an earlier chapter): I prayed, I meditated, and I spent time in quiet reflection. This experience and how I worked through it is further proof that having a grounding practice is invaluable when you most need it.

Third, I took action with Cindy in a timely manner. I didn't confront her immediately after the call because I knew I was angry, and I needed time to find the right words to say. But I also didn't wait days to confront her. We need to take action on things in a timely manner so others can clearly link their words/actions to being confronted about those words/actions. At the end of the day, what I want is for my confrontational but respectful response to change others' behavior, at least in future interactions with me. To do that, others need to be able to cognitively associate their words/actions with the consequence.

Two More Examples of Establishing Boundaries

I recall using the "ouch" technique with another person who was influential in the company. Carol was known for being vicious when things didn't go her way, but no one ever called her out. During one group Zoom conversation, Carol began to roll her eyes and give sarcastic responses to anything I said. I finally said, "Ouch, that one got me, Carol! Clearly you have strong feelings about this issue, so let's take this offline to discuss further. I'll send you a meeting invite." Carol stopped rolling her eyes and remained polite for the duration of the Zoom call.

At the one-on-one meeting with Carol after the Zoom call, I began by saying, "I set up this meeting for us to discuss what happened on the last Zoom call …" Carol cut me off and began to apologize and explain why she had gotten upset. I didn't let her get away with a quick apology. I made her understand the impact of being treated so derisively, the impact on the topic under discussion, etc. I am happy to share that Carol never treated me like that ever again. But her behavior with others remained unchanged. I was one of the few who asserted a boundary with her, so she toed the line with me. It is worth repeating: You will get from others the behavior you accept.

Let me share one final example on the topic of setting boundaries. I was leading a training simulation for executives and senior leaders in my company. The company CEO, known for being a prankster, was a participant in the session. I discovered that the CEO was ignoring some simulation rules and was cheating. I kept calling him out, but he would just laugh and ignore me. The simulation would fail if he kept cheating, so I had to do something. I had major fears about confronting the CEO, but decided it had to be done because it was unfair to the other participants for the simulation to fail. I told myself the worst-case scenario was that I could lose my job, but I'd be able to find another job if I had to. This was my self-pep talk. I also told myself it was a great day to be my last day with that company! With that, on his next cheating attempt, I physically blocked the CEO's path. He kept advancing until we were shoulder to shoulder, and then he began pushing against me, laughing the whole time. I smiled but pushed back against him and told him to quit doing what he was doing. He kept laughing but did play by the rules after that. And I did not lose my job that day! The experience has endured throughout my career as a prime example of when I encountered fear in the workplace and my courage to push past the fear was successful. In similar situations later in my career, to fuel my courage, I often repeated the mantra, "Today is a great day to be my last day in this company!"

Reflection Questions for Establishing and Maintaining Boundaries

Establishing boundaries means ensuring your words and behaviors protect and affirm what matters most to you. It means speaking up or behaving in a way that shows others what you will or will not tolerate as acceptable behavior. Maintaining boundaries is a process that will typically require ongoing effort to sustain those boundaries with others over time. Remember, you will get from others the behavior you accept from them!

- What words/actions by others trigger an adverse and strong reaction in you?

- What are the first signs you notice in your mind or body when you have been triggered?

- When you have been triggered, what specific steps do you take to work through how you have been made to feel, and what process do you use to let go of those feelings?

- What are some specific words you use to establish boundaries with others?

_____

_____

_____

_____

_____

_____

_____

_____

_____

_____

_____

_____

_____

_____

_____

_____

_____

_____

_____

_____

_____

_____

_____

_____

_____

_____

Chapter Six

Harnessing Fear

Fear is a common theme that comes up with coaching clients. No matter who we are or where we are in our careers, we all feel fear at times—it is a normal and unavoidable emotion. The problem is that when we're coming from a place of fear, what we say and how we behave can be counterproductive. In earlier chapters, I outlined why a key to your success as a woman or person of color, is to say yes when presented with opportunities for advancement and greater professional scope. If you feel fear when presented with such an opportunity, and you do not manage that fear, it may cause you to say no to the opportunity. And saying no may prevent future doors from opening. Harnessing and managing fear is a key to your success.

Another reason to learn to control fear as a woman or person of color, is because without getting ahold of your fear, and especially if that fear is disproportionate to the situation, our words and actions may become extreme. We may lash out or have a meltdown when we feel unmanaged fear. Recall, women are more likely to be labeled and penalized for showing their emotions than men—having a meltdown may have far more lasting adverse impact on a woman's reputation than a man's. Also, remember that it is two times more likely for others to comment on a woman's emotional state in the workplace than a man's (McKinsey, 2023). So, while feeling fear may be normal, as a woman or a person of color since you will be held to a different, and at times, higher standard than others, it's important that you learn to manage fear so it doesn't have an adverse long-term impact on your career.

In this chapter, I cover how to recognize fear when it appears, share examples identifying the cause of fear, and present ways to effectively manage fear when it arises so that it doesn't control us or have a detrimental impact on our professional reputation.

Recognizing Fear

People experience fear in different ways, but there are typically some physical and emotional symptoms for each person. Before we can learn to effectively manage our fear, we must learn what fear feels like in our body when it surfaces. For some, fear manifests physically as a rapid heartbeat, sweating, trembling, feeling short of breath, butterflies in the stomach, or tightness in the stomach. Emotionally, we each have our own symptoms of fear. Some get angry, some get upset, while others get a thrill/an adrenaline charge out of it (think of roller coaster fans).

Are you able to clearly recognize how your body responds to the first signs of fear, whether it is from the fear itself or an emotional reaction to that fear? It is important to know how fear manifests in your body because in the workplace, in the midst of normal work encounters, your body will give you physical signals that you are feeling fear well before your logical brain may be able to tell you the same thing. Haven't you seen folks who start to get red in the face or who start to shake when they get upset? The sooner you learn to recognize the physical signs of fear in yourself, the sooner you can be proactive about managing what you say/do in those moments.

Once we've learned to recognize fear when it swells up in us, the next step is to name the fear and learn how to better manage it. To help you do this, I will share some examples of common fears I've heard from clients. We'll take a look at a common scenario where that fear tends to surface, and I'll share some suggestions to address the fear. While this list is not exhaustive, it should serve as a helpful guide to recognize and deal with fear in your own life.

Fear of Being Wrong

In meetings, do you find yourself biting your tongue even when you have things to share? Do you stop yourself from speaking up in case you might be wrong? Think about the consequences of not sharing your thoughts. When I worked with folks who rarely spoke up, I wondered whether they were disengaged, or whether they had nothing to contribute. Either way, these behaviors are likely to prevent employees from getting ahead and certainly won't help maximize their potential career trajectory.

A better way to think about this fear of being wrong is to ask yourself how often you have been wrong in the past and how confident you are that you are correct. Then, think about the potential costs of not speaking up compared to being wrong if you speak up. Observe those who have been successful with their career trajectories in your company. How often do they speak up? Have you ever observed times when they were wrong, and if so, how was it handled by others? You can learn a lot by observing others who are successful in your company. A good ego check is helpful in dealing with this fear—what is the true cost of being wrong when you speak up? Will it cost lives or significant amounts of money? If not, perhaps your ego needs to be harnessed, and you should allow yourself to simply laugh at yourself and learn from the experience if it turns out you are wrong.

Fear of Uncertainty and Change

When there is a potential change in your workplace and there is a lot of uncertainty about how things may play out, do you find yourself fearful of that uncertainty and possible change? What is it about that change that makes you uncomfortable? Be specific. For example, are you worried about losing your status, worried about not being the expert anymore, worried about a new reporting relationship with your team or your direct leader, or some other factors altogether? Go through the exercise of clearly articulating what explicitly is making you uncomfortable so that you can work through that fear.

If you aspire to leadership, having the skill to adapt to change will serve you well. We covered the topic of flexing your tolerance for discomfort earlier in the book. It is normal to feel some emotions when faced with potential changes. Good leaders feel those emotions, but they don't let those emotions incapacitate them, and their recovery rate for dealing with the emotions is rapid.

It is helpful to know the SARA model when dealing with stress and emotional responses. SARA stands for shock, anger, resistance, and acceptance. It is normal for everyone to experience progression along the SARA model when faced with stress. It is also normal to drift back to an earlier step on the model when dealing with stress, meaning a person does not always progress linearly through the phases. Highly successful employees move rapidly through the phases, and perhaps even back and forth through the phases, but they reach the acceptance stage rapidly. Those who are unsuccessful at dealing with change may never arrive at acceptance and may get bogged down in an earlier phase. Think of the example I shared about the woman on the beach who focused on the acrimonious divorce that had taken place eight years prior. She was clearly stuck in a space of resistance to the divorce!

Think about the last professional change you faced and try to recall how long it took you to get through each phase of the SARA model. If you want to accelerate your career trajectory, your goal should be to decrease the amount of time it takes you to work through each of the phases. If you find yourself having to deal with uncertainty and you recognize that you're fearful, remind yourself of the SARA model. Remind yourself that it is normal to feel the emotions of shock, anger, and resistance. But don't allow yourself to get stuck in one of those phases. Do the intentional work with your support system to push yourself to the acceptance stage.

Fear of Not Being Good Enough

Do you consider yourself to be indecisive? Do you find yourself struggling to take action due to a fear of not meeting others' expectations? Do you worry about what others in the workplace think of you? Do you worry they'll think you are not as smart as they once thought, or not as good as their ideal standard?

Why do you give other people so much power over your decisions and actions? How do you really know what others truly think of you? Is it possible you are projecting what they may think, without knowing for sure?

An effective way to work through this fear is to focus on your past successes that demonstrated you did great work. Focus on the acknowledgement you received from others when you did that great work. Repeat their positive words to yourself as a mantra. Analyze the risk of not taking action compared to your fear of not measuring up.

Fear of Failure

Do you find yourself struggling to take action because you are afraid of failure? What if you make a decision and take action but the task/project fails? If you allow this fear to take hold, you will never make decisions or take action.

An effective way to process this fear is to focus on how many successful things you have done in the past, and then consider the risk of not acting compared to the risk of failing if you take action. Which would you regret more deeply? If you "fail" in this situation, what is the consequence? Is it a life-or-death situation or will it cost the company huge amounts of money? It is far more effective to focus on what you will learn, even if you fail. Most likely, you will land on your feet in this company or elsewhere, even if you fail. And if you succeed, think of what that would mean for your career as well as the company.

Fear of Not Being in Control

Do you prefer doing things yourself rather than delegating them to your team to make sure they are "done right?" Do you feel anxious or angry if things do not go according to your plan?

When I was an undergraduate student, I had a roommate who would plan out every aspect of her life. She told me where and exactly how long after graduation she would marry her boyfriend (they were not yet even engaged); how long after the wedding she would get pregnant and have her first child; how long of a gap they would have between their first and second kid, etc. Wow! She was certainly a person who wanted serious control over her life. Even at that age, I knew from my own experience that life does not always turn out as we plan/hope. While this simple example may make it easy to see my former roommate's need for control, I find some clients are unable to see their own need for control in their lives.

If you are rigid in wanting or needing to control all aspects of your professional life, you are setting yourself up for disappointment. There are so many factors beyond your control in the workplace, even when you are an executive. Human dynamics of those on your team, and those you lead, add their own variation to how things unfold.

A better use of your time is to practice giving up control, so you are less averse to not having it in the future. Practice in small ways. If you are a planner, maybe allow other friends to select where and when to have the next dinner outing; if you tend to be the one to insist which route to use to get to a destination, maybe next time, you can let someone else choose the route. And each time you let go in these small ways, take a moment later on to reflect on the outcome and how it made you feel. Hopefully, once you've experienced a few good outcomes, you will be willing to allow bigger decisions to be delegated to others.

Fear of Being Found Out

Have you ever felt like you don't deserve to be in your current position? Do you feel like you lucked out in getting the role, and you don't know as much as you should to be successful? When a person feels like a phony, even though they have had successes in the past, it is known as imposter syndrome. People with imposter syndrome tend to attribute success to external factors (not their own hard work and efforts) but tend to blame failures on their own shortcomings. People with imposter syndrome tend to fear being found out as a phony. In my experience, female clients express this fear more often than my male clients. Male clients may experience the fear, but rarely verbalize it.

It is natural to compare yourself to others. But know that as a woman or person of color, as you climb the ladder, there will be fewer and fewer who look like you. You may be more likely to feel like a phony if you look around the room and you are "the only" or "the first" doing what you are doing. You need to ensure you find productive ways to work through this fear if it emerges, otherwise you will create a self-fulfilling prophecy to justify why you cannot go any higher, or even to justify why you should leave or be asked to leave your position.

If you have imposter syndrome, focus on rapidly building up your technical and career-enhancing competencies. Negotiate for your company to pay for you to work on technical licensure/certifications; ask your company for a leadership coach; and tap deeply and intentionally into your robust support system to boost your confidence.

Fear of Not Being Liked by Influential Others

When you have to make a decision, do you deliberate about options that would please powerful folks in your firm, or do you focus more on following what your data/ analysis suggests as the right decision? Do you have any anxiety about making a decision that influential folks might not like? Have you ever found yourself taking on a new project because you don't want to disappoint your leaders by saying no? Conversely, have you ever refused to take on a new project for fear that if you take it on and aren't successful you will disappoint others? Do you only speak up if you can make a statement others are likely to agree with? Do you censor yourself if you disagree with others so that they won't know you don't agree with their words/actions?

Why are you giving others so much power over your actions, no matter their influence or rank? You don't have to be rude or mean when you express disagreement. But withholding your own thoughts or censoring your actions to please others will take a toll on you emotionally. Why doesn't what you want take precedent over what others might think? Have you asked yourself the core reasons why you prioritize your need to be liked above doing what's best for yourself?

Career success may translate to leadership opportunities being presented to you. And leadership takes courage. It takes courage to speak up for those who cannot, even if it means some peers or senior leaders may not like you for it; courage to take a stand against decisions that violate your values; courage to be willing to say what others may not. As you climb up the leadership ranks, your perspective as a woman or person of color will likely be distinct from mainstream leaders in your firm because you have had different and unique life and professional experiences. Any benefits to having a diverse leadership team are only realized if those of us with these diverse perspectives are willing to share them, even if those perspectives aren't popular. If you worry about being liked by others and are afraid of disappointing others, eventually you could find yourself surrounded by peers who have very different values than your own and you could find yourself implementing decisions you don't agree with. In short, you could find yourself in a workplace where you aren't being authentic to yourself or your values.

Tactics to Harness Fear When It Is Stirred Up

It wouldn't be feasible to list every fear in the section above, and my suggestions above may not fit every situation or work for every individual. For these reasons, I want to share more general tactics to manage fear, so you have some practical tips to try no matter the situation.

When you recognize through physical symptoms that fear has been triggered in you, first analyze what has made you fearful. In other words, begin by trying to name your fear. The list of fears above can be used as a guide to help you get started. Naming it will help you understand what is needed to get through it. Second, give yourself grace. Don't berate yourself for having the fear, or even for being mired in the fear if you've had it for a long time. You now know the fear is there, and you will be able to work through it! Be patient with yourself.

Third, spend time to prepare words and behaviors you can use when you recognize fear is making you feel anxious. When we are fearful, we don't make good decisions so find ways to buy yourself time if pushed to make a decision. Say something like "Let me think about it and I'll get back to you" or "I need time to process this information." Tell yourself to breathe and stay calm, and then focus on slow, deep breathing or whatever practice you normally use to calm yourself down.

To overcome the fear, a great tactic is to recount how often you have successfully overcome other fears. This is a simple but powerful exercise: Complete this sentence about every past fear that you have overcome. "If I had given in to that fear, I would never have …" Your answer could be things you learned, people you met, or maybe great experiences you had all because you were able to overcome each fear. As an illustration, if I had to do the exercise I might say, "If I had given in to the fear of relocating for a job, I would never have experienced the successive promotions and incredible professional growth!"

Completing exercises like focusing on how you successfully overcame other fears will help fuel your faith in yourself so that you can overcome the current fear as well. Studies show that optimism about the past makes you more optimistic about the future. That optimism will fuel your ability to get through the current fear.

When I work with clients on processing fear, once they gain an awareness of those fears, they usually experience resentment of the situation and the people around them. It is a waste of your energy to dwell in the resentment. Instead, use your energy to understand why you gave your power up to others, decide how you want/need to be different in the future, and begin to practice being the new you. If you're unable to do this, you'll be stuck in negativity and resentment, and that is the energy you will put out into the world. Don't be that divorced woman I met on the Florida beach! Remember, your energy attracts/repels people. When people see you as fearful and closed, it repels them. It is a self-fulfilling prophecy. The more fearful you are that others will not like you or that you will fail, the more likely those things will actually come true, because that's the energy you are putting out. Don't dwell in resentment, it will only repel those around you.

What else can you do to overcome fear?

- Get quiet. Get quiet and spend time alone in reflection so you can name the fear and work to overcome it.

- Choose joy. Pursue things that give you joy and fuel your growth, even if you are unsure where it will all lead or what others will think of you. For example, if you enjoy painting, take art classes even if painting has nothing to do with your professional career. Living free of fear means you don't waste precious energy worrying about what others think or feel about your choices.

- Pivot to gratitude. Gratitude helps us be more compassionate with ourselves. When I begin to worry about something, if I force myself to list three to five things for which I am grateful in that moment, I notice a significant decrease in the hold the thing I'm worried about has on me.

- Learn to laugh at yourself when fear surfaces. Don't be surprised when fear comes up. Instead, laugh at how quickly you forget your past successes and succumbed to fear. This should help you stop taking things so seriously. Develop your own version of "today is a great day to be my last day in this company!" Use it as a mantra to repeat when you notice the first signs of fear.

- Ask for help from your support system. Ask for help from God/the universe/your angels if that is what you believe in.

Reflection Questions for Harnessing Fear

Although we all feel fear at times, if we don't manage fear in the workplace, what we say and how we behave can be counterproductive. It is important to recognize the physical signs of fear when they appear, identify its cause, and effectively manage it so it doesn't have a detrimental impact on your professional success.

- How does your body react when you experience fear?

- What fears have you successfully overcome in the past? What did you learn as a result of overcoming those fears?

- Do you have any current fears that are constraining your professional growth? What specific actions are you taking to overcome these fears?

Chapter Seven

Being Authentic to Yourself

Any leadership book you pick up will have a section about how your success depends on being authentic, meaning showing up fully as your true self in the professional setting. Being told to be authentic is all well and good, but for those of us in the minority, for those of us who are women, people of color, or both, we have to take that advice with a grain of salt. In my own case, and for many of my female clients and clients of color, we may have either experienced negative reactions when we showed up fully in the workplace, or we may have observed others being treated negatively when they showed up fully in the workplace. The challenge for us is to balance the tension of being authentic in the workplace, while feeling safe enough to do so. My suggestion is that as a woman or person of color, one key to your success is to be authentic, *in your own way*.

The cost of not being able to be fully authentic in the workplace comes in the form of a huge emotional toll.

I base that statement on my personal experience as well as published research. If you feel the need to hide aspects of yourself, or change your behavior or language in the workplace, it has an emotional impact. We only resort to such actions because we don't feel psychologically safe; we resort to those actions because we don't feel like we fully belong in our work environments. It is exhausting to always have your guard up! It cumulatively translates to an adverse impact on productivity and your professional level of engagement in that environment. Here we are, working hard to be successful in our roles, while simultaneously having to overcome feelings of not belonging. We're working twice as hard to overcome those feelings, strive to be productive, and still be as successful as those who innately feel like they belong. We are unnecessarily expending all that energy.

I want you to understand the emotional toll it takes for you not to be authentic. And then I want you to consciously determine how to be authentic *in your own way*. By making that conscious choice, choose also to let go of the emotional toll if you cannot fully be yourself in the workplace. Instead, take pride in the fact that you can choose to be authentic in your own way, revealing only what you eles to share with others in the workplace, and let that conscious choice free you from adversely impacting your engagement level or productivity. And if you happen to be in a work environment where you can fully be yourself, celebrate it!

Another cost of not being authentic in the workplace is that it may prevent others from developing a deep relationship with you. If others don't know much about you, and especially if they sense you are aloof or withholding more about yourself, they are unlikely to feel a genuine connection or affection for you. And as discussed in the positivity chapter, people hire those they like. Folks need to feel like they know you well enough to like you before they will tap you for promotions.

How We May Have Learned to Adjust Our Behavior and Language

The negative experiences we encounter when we've shown up fully or observed others showing up fully are what teach us to modify our behavior and language in the workplace. Here are some examples of negative experiences:

- When I tell others I grew up in Africa, folks have made jokes that I must have worn a loincloth and ridden an elephant to school.

- When they learn my parents are from India, many people assume I must practice Hinduism and be a vegetarian.

- When I tell people that I only get to see my sister in Zambia once every year or two, some folks respond by saying, "but you get to spend two weeks with her when you see her" or "at least you can use Zoom to see her." These comments seem hypocritical from folks who spend time with their own extended family multiple times every month, and during every holiday. During the COVID-19 shutdown, when families were told to isolate, these were the same folks who were distraught despite having Zoom to visit with their loved ones. The same ones who had little empathy that the pandemic had extended my in-person time away from my sister well beyond two years!

- When my African-American friends and clients reveal they occasionally may wear a wig, they get comments about being lucky to never have a bad hair day, and are asked what they "really" look like.

The negative experiences people encounter when they've shown up fully or observed others showing up fully can result in the use of covering or code switching. Covering is what happens when people hide some aspects of themselves to better fit in with their surroundings. They consciously choose to omit sharing things about themselves for their own safety or because they have seen others being treated poorly for sharing similar things. For example, in my neighborhood, there is a blatantly racist homeowner. Another neighbor, whose husband is Hispanic but passes for White, deliberately doesn't reveal her last name to the racist homeowner, knowing it will change how that homeowner treats their family.

Code switching happens when we behave differently based on the group we are with. A simple example is when we use a more formal way of speaking in the workplace, but use slang and more colorful language with our friends. Before we examine the impact of covering and code switching, below are some examples of what the concepts look like in practice.

- I was very selective about personal items that were displayed in any company office in which I worked. I didn't display photos of loved ones, friends, or anything identifying the religion I practice.

- During COVID-19 when everyone had to work from home, I intentionally blurred my background so that nothing in my home office was visible to others. Other clients of color have shared this same sentiment.

- African-American clients have shared how carefully they choose their hairstyle for the workplace. They are cautious about any style that could be perceived as "too" culturally specific.

- I've had clients who adjusted their speech pattern and even tried to adjust their accent to better fit within their workplace. As someone who has an accent and grew up outside of the US, I understand their perspective. People inevitably comment on or ask about my accent when they first meet me. While I've been told I have an accent that makes anything I say sound "smarter," I consciously choose not to change my accent even though having one makes me stand out. My accent is an artifact of my lived experiences, and it matters to me to be authentic with it.

- I found myself covering when I first moved to Tennessee because I was shocked at the number of folks who told stories about going to the gun range or shopping for ammunition on weekends. I have strong negative feelings about guns because my family experienced a home invasion by armed thieves when I was twelve years old. I never shared that story in the workplace, but I also consciously avoided saying how I feel about guns.

Psychological Safety

When working with clients on the topic of authenticity, we focus on the concept of psychological safety. Dr. Amy Edmondson is *the* expert on this topic and has written numerous books and articles about it. As a woman or a person of color, or both, you need to understand what impacts psychological safety so you can recognize it when you see it, but also know how to create it within your own teams.

According to Dr. Edmondson, psychological safety is the belief that you will not be punished or humiliated for speaking up with ideas or concerns. It is the belief that even if you make a mistake, you will not be punished or humiliated. When I work with clients who cover or code switch, we work together to determine how much of an emotional toll that takes, and I challenge the client to uncover the root of their fear of speaking up by asking them the following questions. What specific thing(s) happened when they or someone they observed spoke up, and where and when did it take place? I want the client to analyze whether the environment has changed since that event(s) took place, and if appropriate, to begin to work on letting go and moving forward.

The results of research in this area clearly state that learning cannot take place when psychological safety is low. To learn you need to be able to absorb new information and try new things. The absence of psychological safety means the fear of making mistakes will keep you from trying new things! The more successful you are, the more likely you'll be asked to take on new things, so if you want to accelerate your career trajectory, ideally, you want to be in an environment where you have psychological safety. Or in the absence of psychological safety, you need to know how to cope in the environment.

Your direct leader sets the tone for the level of psychological safety you feel. They are not the sole determinant of how much safety you may feel, but they are a big part of it. The words and actions of your leader create the climate within the team, which in turn impacts the mindset and behaviors of their team members. Great leaders are humble and demonstrate vulnerability, and they invite the participation of their team members. Ineffective leaders are arrogant and don't like to lose face. Ineffective leaders won't accept responsibility for failure, and may mock or belittle any suggestions they don't like. Ineffective leaders are slow to express gratitude and have long memories, never forgetting anyone who crossed them or made a mistake. Ineffective leaders are threatened by strong team members and take credit for others' work.

If you have a leader who makes you feel psychologically unsafe, assess whether your current role and current company will help you achieve your long-term goals. As you practice handling that leader, you must work equally hard not to feel trapped. You must not allow yourself to feel you have no other options. Why? Like I said in the chapter about boundaries, feeling trapped will negatively impact your ability to set boundaries. If you have a leader who makes you feel psychologically unsafe, and there is no other strategic professional reason for you to stay in your current role and current company, it is time to leave.

I recall one specific instance in my career where I made such a decision. At the time, I reported to an extremely ineffective leader. This leader was arrogant, demanding, slow to give gratitude, easily intimidated by others, and harbored long-lasting grudges. While I liked the company I worked for, seeing this leader being rewarded for ineffective leadership did make me question the company and its actual values. After a year witnessing multiple ways in which the leader demonstrated how little they cared about me, I knew it was time to begin an external job search. It was time for me to leave that leader.

Around the same time, I was chosen to participate in a company workshop. During the workshop, we participated in a privilege walk exercise. That exercise left me deeply distressed because at the end of the exercise, participants who were female or of color were still at or close to the starting line, while almost all the white, male participants were at the complete opposite side of the room from the starting line. The exercise was a tangible demonstration of just how far apart we were as women and people of color compared to where the white men in the company were! During the debrief, the workshop facilitator asked me to share why the exercise upset me. For the first time in my tenure with the company, I was completely honest about not being seen, not feeling like I belonged in the company, and not feeling like my leaders cared about or valued me. It was that speech from the heart that opened doors for me after the workshop and changed my reporting structure to a different, amazing leader. But the only reason I was able to give that speech was because mentally I already had one foot out of the door, so there was little perceived risk in me speaking the truth.

Don't underestimate the impact of not having psychological safety. If you have a leader who makes you feel psychologically unsafe, and there is no other strategic professional reason for you to stay in your current role and current company, it is time to leave.

How to Be Authentic in Your Own Way

I want you to consciously choose how to be authentic *in your own way.* Authenticity does not have to be all-or-nothing. You can choose selectively when and how to show up fully. If you want to show up more fully, but the environment around you doesn't allow it, don't deplete your emotional bank to do so. Focus instead on the reasons you are consciously choosing to remain in that environment. Focus on the control you have over *that* choice.

If the cause of your reluctance to show up fully is due to negative past experiences, perhaps you can practice showing up more fully with select colleagues, when you feel doing so will have little perceived associated risks. In those situations where you receive no bad reaction/feedback, choose to show up a little more fully in the future in those safe spaces with those colleagues. Revealing more about who you are to select colleagues will allow you to develop deeper friendships with them. The literature supports the idea that when we have deeper relationships with at least some of our colleagues at work, it correspondingly increases our level of engagement and satisfaction. Finding such safe havens where you can be more unguarded should increase your work satisfaction, which in turn should offset some of the emotional drain from not being able to be your whole self with the entire firm.

What does it mean when I say you can choose selectively when and how to show up fully in the workplace? While my race is visible to others, I rarely reveal my religion, marital/family status, or even dietary norms in the workplace. But because of the way I look, many people assume I must practice Hinduism and be a vegetarian. If we have a meaningful professional relationship, you will learn more about how and where I was raised, the religion I practice, my family and my dietary norms, but until then I do nothing to address assumptions. In other words, I choose when, and with whom, I reveal more about myself.

For folks who don't have a close professional relationship with me, through my behavior and actions, they will see me consistently demonstrate my values. And it is a tactic that has served me well and has allowed me to be authentic to myself even when I don't feel free to show other aspects of myself in the workplace. You do not have to compromise your values even if you have strategic reasons to stay in a company where you cannot show up fully. I encourage you to be authentic in your own way, by being true to yourself and demonstrating your values.

In one company where I worked, the CEO would often comment in public about what an amazing employee I was and how well I exemplified the values of the firm. This was relatively early in my tenure at the firm, and I'd never worked on any projects with the CEO, so I was confused about how he could possibly know me well enough to make such comments. I finally asked the CEO one day how he knew my values. He told me he saw my values in action early one morning when I walked into the office building.

I remember the occasion well. I would normally get to the office early, well before most employees, and well before the main lobby receptionist. On one specific morning as I walked in, I saw a visitor in the lobby, but none of the reception desk staff had arrived yet. While it wasn't my job to handle visitors, I wanted the person to feel seen, welcomed, and received, so I approached the visitor to ensure their host was aware they were waiting. The visitor had been taken care of, so I turned around to take the elevator up to my office. Unbeknownst to me, the CEO was just a few feet behind me and had seen the entire exchange. He smiled at me, and we rode up in the elevator together. My actions that morning made me stand out to the CEO in a lasting fashion. In subsequent years, as I rose through the ranks, I worked closely with that CEO on various initiatives. Other senior leaders always commented on how much the CEO respected and liked me. The CEO had become my executive sponsor because he observed me demonstrate my values that one morning in the lobby.

Final Words of Advice on Authenticity Your Own Way

As a woman or person of color, one of the seven keys to success is being authentic to yourself. My suggestion is to make the conscious choice about how much to reveal about yourself, and with whom, based on your work environment. That means I cannot tell you prescriptively how to be your own version of authentic, only *you* can. I cannot tell you what will take an emotional toll on you. I can only tell you that paying the toll is depleting your energy and taking energy away from reaching your potential and achieving your best professional life.

In this chapter I've shared examples of why I and others have chosen to hide aspects of ourselves, and ways I and others have achieved the balance between being just authentic enough for others to connect with us in the workplace, while keeping ourselves psychologically safe. I hope you see you are not alone, and that this chapter has given you some suggestions about how to achieve balance in your life.

Reflection Questions for Being Authentic to Yourself

As a woman or person of color, one key to your success is to be authentic, *in your own way*. If you cannot fully be yourself in the workplace, find ways to release the emotional toll this takes on you. Instead, take pride in the fact that you choose to be authentic in your own way, revealing only what you choose to share with others in the workplace.

- Do you feel an emotional toll from covering at work? What active things are you doing to reduce that emotional toll?

- Name specific people at work with whom you have a safe haven to be yourself. If you need to build/ enhance your safe haven, what steps are you taking to find these coworkers?

- If we polled leaders in your firm, what values might they attribute to you based on your behavior and words?

_____

_____

_____

_____

_____

_____

_____

_____

_____

_____

_____

_____

_____

_____

_____

_____

_____

_____

_____

_____

_____

_____

_____

Workbook

Taking Action

At the beginning of the book, I recommended that you document your thoughts, ideas, questions, and concerns as you worked through each chapter of the book. For this next part, carve out some time, free from distractions. Then, revisit your notes from earlier chapters, and develop a strategic plan to implement the tools and strategies you have learned to successfully navigate your professional environment and elevate yourself to the next level. In its simplest form, your strategic plan is nothing more than being able to articulate what you will do, by when, to achieve the action items listed in your notes. Identify the areas where you know you will need assistance or additional resources. List your ideas about those individuals in your support system who can provide the assistance and additional resources you need to research to take the next steps. The final portion of this chapter provides some high-level questions to help guide you through this section.

Do not put the book away without taking action! Do not walk away from developing your personal strategic plan for advancement. As I said, reading the book was a big step in the right direction. How you take action after reading the book determines how soon or whether you will shatter your own glass ceiling. You must prioritize yourself because no one else will do it for you. You can do this!

From working with coaching clients, I know this is the point at which fatigue and frustration can easily set in unless you consciously take steps to prevent it from happening. Go back and re-read the chapter on tenacity. Go back and read your notes about how you have overcome past trials and prevailed. Reliving those memories will energize you for the strategic plan development stage. This is also the stage at which you should rely heavily on your leadership coach or your professional support system to keep you focused, keep you accountable for sticking to your timetable for deliverables, and keep you energized and motivated to continue working on yourself. You can do this! Take a deep breath, smile and congratulate yourself for how far you have come already in your career, smile that you are at this strategic stage, and dive in! I cannot wait to see what you will achieve next!

Action Questions for Your Personal Strategic Plan

I recommend tackling one section below at a time. Whether you work on each section on your own, with your personal board of directors, or with your coach, document your ideas and commitments from each section so that you can assess your progress over time.

Your Commitment to Yourself

At a very high level, what commitment will you make to yourself as a result of reading this book? What will you do, by when, because you picked up this book, read it, and followed through by completing the action steps at the end of each chapter?

Tenacity Enhancement

If you'd like to have more tenacity, what action steps are you taking to grow it? What is your commitment to yourself to enhance your tenacity, and how will you know when you have achieved your ideal level?

Your Practice

What is your regular practice (meditation, prayer, quiet reflection time, etc.)? How much time do you prioritize for this practice? After reading this book, will you make any changes to the practice, its duration, or frequency?

What are some of the ways in which you express gratitude in the workplace? Do you feel the need to develop additional ways to express gratitude?

Grow Your Expertise and Credibility

Are you an expert in your field? Are you someone others turn to for advice and recommendations? If not, what specific formal education will you pursue, or conferences will you attend, by when, to enhance your expertise? What opportunities does your organization offer to pay for your education/conferences?

Say Yes to More

What professional projects can you volunteer to take on that are outside your current scope? How will you increase your chances of succeeding with those specific projects if they are assigned to you?

Unstick Any Blocks

Have you had any professional setbacks that left you stuck? Whose help will you seek to help you let go and learn from those setbacks? What ideas do you have about how to let go of the setbacks?

Personal Development Commitment

What is your top goal for your personal development? What have you read or listened to most recently for your own growth and development? How often are you reading or listening to books and articles? If you feel you don't currently have time to work on your own development, what specific steps will you take to remedy that?

Negotiating for Yourself

What aspects of your compensation package or perks do you want to renegotiate? With whom will you practice your negotiation communication in a factual, data-driven way? When will you request a meeting to begin the renegotiation process?

Shore up Your Support System

Who is on your support system? If your personal board of directors lacks diversity and seasoned members, what is your specific plan to recruit new members?

Do you have a leadership coach? If not, do you need one? How will you find a leadership coach who will challenge and support you?

Developing Better Boundaries

Where in your professional life do you need to set better boundaries? Do you need to say no to anyone or give up any professional responsibilities that are no longer serving you? With whom will you practice how to say no in a calm, assertive, and non-defensive way?

Harness Any Fears

From the chapter on fear, which of the outlined fears are real for you? What specific things are you going to do to process each fear you face? How will you know when you have overcome or at least developed better ways to manage each fear?

Assess Your Current Psychological Safety

How psychologically safe is your work environment? If you feel unsafe, what privilege does your current job/ current organization afford you that justifies staying where you are? If there are no privileges for staying, what keeps you from leaving? If there are no privileges to staying, have a conversation with a member of your personal board of directors or your coach about how to move past inertia and look for another job.

The Energy You Exude

How would you describe the energy you exude? When people spend time with you, do they leave energized or more subdued? After reading this book, what kind of energy do you want to consciously exude, and how will you create that energy in yourself?

Conclusion

Closing Thoughts

You are not alone. Your struggle is not unique. I hope this book has helped you truly see that. I hope you saw yourself in the stories I shared. And I hope the tactics/suggestions have already begun to help you overcome and learn from any challenges you are facing on your professional journey.

While women and people of color are still the minority in senior leadership positions, if we collectively work on ourselves, if we collectively make ourselves a priority, we can change things. You made an investment in yourself by reading this book. What you do next determines how much more you continue to make yourself a priority. Reading the book was a step in the right direction. How you take action after reading the book determines how soon or whether you will shatter your own glass ceiling.

Finally, be kind to yourself. Be gentle with yourself. You invested your time and energy in reading this book and processing various reflection exercises. Celebrate your investment in yourself. Manifest how using the tips and tactics you learned and using what you learned or affirmed about yourself, you will elevate your career trajectory and shatter any glass ceiling that is holding you back.

You can do it! You are not alone. I believe in you.

Reference List

Babcock, Linda, and Sara Laschever. 2021. *Women Don't Ask: Negotiation and the Gender Divide*. Princeton University Press.

Brooks, Arthur, C. 2022. *From Strength to Strength: Finding Success, Happiness, and Deep Purpose in the Second Half of Life*. Portfolio/Penguin.

Clark, Dorie. 2018. "How Women Can Develop—and Promote—Their Personal Brand." *Harvard Business Review*.

Edmondson, Amy, C. 2018. *The Fearless Organization: Creating Psychological Safety in the Workplace for Learning, Innovation, and Growth*. John Wiley & Sons.

Ellsworth, Diana, Ruth Imrose, Holly Price, and Nicolette Rainone. 2022. "Why Women of Color Are Leaving, and How to Rethink Your DE&I Strategy." January 24, 2022, *McKinsey & Company*.

Frank, Lydia. 2015. "How the Gender Pay Gap Widens as Women Get Promoted." *Harvard Business Review*, November 2015.

Norman, Steven M., Bruce J. Avolio, and Fred Luthans. 2010. "The Impact of Positivity and Transparency on Trust in Leaders and Their Perceived Effectiveness." *The Leadership Quarterly*, Vol 21(3), June 2010, pp 350-364.

McKinsey & Company. 2023. "*Women in the Workplace Report.*"

Schaeffer, Katherine. 2023. "The Data on Women Leaders" September 27, 2023, <u>*Pew Research Center*</u> *Social Trends Fact Sheet*.

Ready, Douglas A., Jay A. Conger, and Linda A. Hill. 2010. "Are You a High Potential?" *Harvard Business Review*, June 2010.

About the Author

Vinitia Mathews provides meaningful career support to elevate and propel women and people of color. She helps individuals unearth their leadership hurdles and effectively overcome them. She believes women and people of color need support, encouragement, and specific techniques to elevate their voice to make the professional world more equitable and inclusive.

Vinitia has been instrumental in creating inclusive cultures in organizations ranging from ten thousand to over fifty thousand employees across multiple states. She has served as an officer and senior vice president of multibillion-dollar for-profit organizations and been a key operational leader in enhancing employee engagement and leadership development within publicly traded, private, private equity-owned, and nonprofit systems. Vinitia has two decades of healthcare operational experience and a decade of experience as a management consultant and executive leadership coach serving multiple industries.

Vinitia holds a PhD in strategic management and an MBA in healthcare management from Texas Tech University. To contact Vinitia for leadership coaching or speaking engagements, reach out to her via her website at www.sageleadersolutions.com

www.ingramcontent.com/pod-product-compliance
Lightning Source LLC
Chambersburg PA
CBHW040858210326
41597CB00029B/4886